A Window into
Orthodox Christianity

A Window into
Orthodox Christianity

Nicolas Kazarian

Translated by Lianna Sanford Kazarian

Foreword
by
His Eminence Archbishop Elpidophoros of America

HOLY CROSS
ORTHODOX PRESS
Brookline, Massachusetts

Originally published in French as: *L'orthodoxie*
© 2018, Éditions *Eyrolles*, Paris, France
English Translation © Nicolas Kazarian, 2024

Published by

Holy Cross Orthodox Press
Hellenic College, Inc.
50 Goddard Avenue
Brookline, MA 02445

All rights reserved. No part of this book may be used or reproduced in any manner whatsoever without written permission, except in the case of brief quotations embodied in critical articles and reviews. For more information contact Holy Cross Orthodox Press.

Picture Credits

St. Nicholas Church: Alan Karchmer
The Pantokraton: Saint Nicholas National Shrine
Fr. Kazarian: GOA/Sotiris Michalatos

ISBN 978-1-935317-10-4

Publisher's Cataloging-in-Publication
(Provided by Cassidy Cataloguing Services, Inc.)
Names: Kazarian, Nicolas, author. | Kazarian, Lianna Sanford, translator. | Elpidophoros, Archbishop, writer of foreword.
Title: A window into Orthodox Christianity / Nicolas Kazarian ; translated by Lianna Sanford Kazarian ; foreword by His Eminence Archbishop Elpidophoros of America.
Other titles: Orthodoxie. English
Description: Brookline, Massachusetts : Holy Cross Orthodox Press, [2024] | "Originally published in French as: L'orthodoxie (Paris : Éditions Eyrolles, 2019."--Title page verso. | Includes bibliographical references.
Identifiers: ISBN: 978-1-935317-10-4
Subjects: LCSH: Orthodox Eastern Church--History. | Orthodox Eastern Church--Doctrines. | Fathers of the church. | Orthodox Eastern Church--Liturgy. | Icons. | Spirituality--Orthodox Eastern Church.
Classification: LCC: BX320.3 .K39 2025 | DDC: 281.9--dc23

*To my parents, Rev. Pierre and Pres. Hélène
& to Pres. Lianna, Matthias and Emilie*

In memory of my brother Serge

Contents

Foreword
His Eminence Archbishop Elpidophoros xi

Prologue xiii

Introduction xvii

| **PART 1** | **The History of the Orthodox Church** .... **1** |

Chapter 1 | The Early Church 3

Chapter 2 | Unity in the Byzantine Empire,
Division Among Christians 13

Chapter 3 | From the Fall of Constantinople to Today 25

| **PART 2** | **The Heart of Orthodoxy** .... **41** |

Chapter 4 | Orthodox Doctrine...43

Chapter 5 | The Church Fathers.......................................57

Chapter 6 | A Communion of Churches.................................69

| **PART 3** | **Orthodox Worship** .... **85** |

Chapter 7 | Orthodox Worship Services................................87

Chapter 8 | Icons 101

Chapter 9 | Spirituality 111

Further Reading 125

I give you a new commandment, that you love one another.
Just as I have loved you, you also should love one another.

John 13:34

Foreword

In the pages that follow, the reader will find a concise and rewarding history and overview of the Holy Orthodox Church, which describes and illuminates God's salvific and providential love for the world. The author, Protopresbyter Nicolas Kazarian, informs his work through his extensive ecumenical and pastoral experience, thus creating a compendium of the Orthodox Christian faith that is as beneficial for the seeker as it is for the faithful. I express my gratitude to Father Nicolas and to his beloved spouse and translator, Presvytera Lianna Kazarian, for offering this erudite and efficient work for the good of all.

As Orthodox Christianity remains a minority Christian expression in the Western World, Father Kazarian's clear and comprehensive survey is one more knowledge arrow in the quiver of growing literature that is bringing our holy faith to the awareness of the surrounding culture. The book is a concise text that is as accessible as it is accurate. History, aesthetics, liturgy, theology, key persons, and events punctuate the text and create the "window" of which the title speaks. The window is clear and wide, revealing the vast landscape of history that spans the two millennia of the Church's march through time. This insightful text is sure to enlighten and inform many both within and without the Church.

I heartily encourage the wide distribution and reading of *A Window into Orthodox Christianity*, and commend Father Nicolas for bringing his original French offering (through Presvytera's translation) into the English language. I have no doubt that many souls will profit from the clarity, organization, and scope of the text. As they gaze through this window, they will find many perspectives with which to view the multiform horizons of Orthodox Christianity. And in these lines of sight, they will behold the vision of our Lord Jesus Christ and His Holy Church, which is His Body and the living temple of His continuing presence on earth.

†ELPIDOPHOROS
Archbishop of America
Sunday of Orthodoxy, 2024.

| Prologue

In the intricate tapestry of human history, certain threads stand out as luminous beacons, weaving through time and culture to illuminate the path of faith. Among these threads, Orthodox Christianity emerges as a rich and profound religious tradition, offering spiritual nourishment to countless souls across centuries and continents.

As we embark on this journey through the heart of Orthodox Christianity, the best hidden treasure in the American religious landscape, we invite you into a world of ancient wisdom, vibrant traditions, and timeless truths. Originally published in French in 2018, this introductory exploration is now presented in English, adapted for an American audience unversed in the nuances of Orthodox Christianity. This edition seeks to unravel the mysteries of a tradition that has withstood the test of time, transcending cultural boundaries to touch and transform the lives of believers and seekers alike.

For those who are unfamiliar with the treasure of Orthodox Christianity, this book serves as a gentle guide, unraveling its complexities with clarity and simplicity. Whether you approach these pages with a curious mind, a skeptical heart, or an earnest search for spiritual grounding, our aim is to provide a bridge into the profound beauty and depth of Orthodox Christian theology, liturgy and life.

In the pages that follow, we will traverse the ancient corridors of Byzantium, stand in awe before the icons that adorn sacred spaces, and contemplate the profound theological insights that have shaped the minds of theologians and saints. From the majestic chants that resonate through centuries-old domes to the intimate practices that define the daily lives of Orthodox Christians, we will open a window into a hallowed reality.

This English translation is more than a linguistic adaptation; it is an endeavor to present the essence of Orthodox Christianity in a way that resonates with the cultural nuances of the American experience. As such, this book is inspired in a large measure by the unique leadership of His Eminence Archbishop Elpidophoros of America, whom I thank for his blessing.

I wish to express here my deepest gratitude to my wife, Presbytera Lianna Kazarian, for undertaking this important translation project while supporting so many other aspects of our family, professional and pastoral lives. This project would never have seen the light of day without her unwavering trust. In this confidence, she was joined by our two wonderful children Matthias and Emilie, as well as by my beloved parents Rev. Protopresbyter Pierre Kazarian and Presbytera Hélène Kazarian, MD.

Gratitude is a cornerstone of any collaborative endeavor, and as I present this current version, I want to recognize the person whose idea of an English version inspired this volume, my dear friend Rev. Protopresbyter Alexandre Sadkowski. I extend my heartfelt thanks to those whose dedication and support have brought this project to fruition by their inspiration and presence: His All-Holiness Ecumenical Patriarch Bartholomew, His Eminence Elder-Metropolitan Emmanuel of Chalcedon, Rev. John Chryssavgis and Rev. Nicholas Anton. Additionally, my sincere thanks extend to all my colleagues at the Greek Orthodox Archdiocese of America and especially those from the Inter-Orthodox, Ecumenical and Interfaith Department: Spyridoula, Niki, Hannah, Ana, Antony, Maria, Harry and Alex. To the many partners I have encountered during my ecumenical and interfaith journey and who have generously shared their passion for faith and service, they have enriched these pages with the authenticity that only true friendship can impart.

Finally, may this work stand as a token of appreciation and dedication to all the beloved members of Saint Eleftherios Greek Orthodox Church in New York City, whom I have the honor to serve.

Introduction

The Orthodox Church is one of the three great traditions that make up Christianity today, alongside Catholicism and Protestantism. While it is the smallest in number of these three traditions, with some 350 million members worldwide, it is also the oldest. The Orthodox Church affirms its continuity with the undivided traditions of the early Church. With its historic and geographical roots in the eastern Mediterranean, it sees itself as the guardian of the cradle of the Scriptures, the places where Jesus lived, and the region where the Apostles first evangelized: in Jerusalem, Antioch, Alexandria, Rome, and beyond. The Orthodox Church also considers itself the heir and the guarantor of Christian doctrine as it was formulated by the Fathers and Councils of the first millennium, following the conversion of the Roman Empire. After developing along the Mediterranean coast and spreading northwards into Europe, Christianity continued to look eastwards. Orthodoxy expanded its influence into the Slavic lands of Eastern Europe before growing worldwide as twentieth century conflicts and the resulting waves of migration redrew the Orthodox ecclesial map on a global scale. In the twentieth century, Orthodoxy became a major presence in the West, even as it suffered persecution in the East, particularly behind the Iron Curtain. Even so, it remains largely unfamiliar outside its traditional heartlands. What lies behind the exotic aesthetics of icons, golden domes, bearded clergy, and long services? The answer is right there in its name. The word "Orthodoxy," from the Greek *orthos*, "right," and *doxa*, "glorification" and/or "belief," refers to a double reality: believing rightly and worshiping rightly. This articulation of faith and worship is characteristic of the Orthodox approach. With its unique theology, and confessing Christ as man and God, and God as the Trinity, Father, Son, and Holy Spirit, Orthodoxy advances a holistic vision of Creation, its role in society, and even its organization. The Orthodox Church is a communion of fifteen local autocephalous (independent) churches, united in the image of the Trinity. This vision of unity reflects what, on the spiritual level, it calls holiness: an experience of the Gospel message as union with God in the human person. Theologians refer to such holiness as deification or *theosis*. *Theosis* depends on the salvation brought by Christ and experienced through the sacraments in the communal life of the Church.

The Orthodox Church as we know it today developed in three major phases.

| Orthodoxy in the first millennium

The Orthodox Church originated with the emergence of the first Christian communities in Jerusalem after the death, resurrection, and ascension of Jesus Christ. Early Christianity, which gradually broke away from Judaism while opening up to converts from paganism, made the celebration of the Eucharist, in which the Body and Blood of Christ are distributed in the form of bread and wine, the core of Christian identity. Over the next three centuries, the liturgical and dogmatic foundations of Christianity were laid down by the Gospels and the first Apostolic writings, and later the works of the early Apologetic Fathers, which would inspire the subsequent development of Christianity. In 313 AD, the Emperor Constantine ended the Roman Empire's persecution of Christians. Christianity's increasing influence brought about a need for a deeper understanding of its teachings. This was achieved by the seven ecumenical councils held between 325 and 787.

After the Schism of 1054

During the first millennium, Christianity was united around five great churches: Rome, Constantinople, Alexandria, Antioch, and Jerusalem. Over time, however, dissensions between Rome and Constantinople, the two capitals of the Roman Empire, led to an estrangement and ultimately a schism between Eastern and Western Christianity. The antagonism between East and West deepened when Constantinople was sacked during the Fourth Crusade in 1204. In the centuries that followed, it became clear that the split was irreversible, despite a series of attempts at reunification. After the fall of the Byzantine Empire in 1453, Orthodoxy's center of gravity gradually shifted from Constantinople to Moscow.

The majority of Slavic peoples had become Orthodox following the baptism of Kyiv in 988. Even today, the majority of Orthodox Christians live in Russia, Ukraine, and neighboring countries.

Orthodoxy in the twentieth century and beyond

The bloody wars and revolutions of the twentieth century brought turmoil and suffering to the Orthodox Church. Persecution in the Soviet Union, and later in its satellite states, drove many Orthodox Christians into exile in Western Europe, particularly France, as well as the United States and Australia. Successive waves of migration from Eastern and Southeastern Europe redrew the map of Orthodoxy worldwide, adding a "diaspora" to its traditional territory. The new social and political environment that Orthodox immigrants found in the West sparked an intense theological and spiritual renaissance, as they sought answers to the questions raised by their encounter with religious pluralism, democracy, and secularization.

Entering the twenty-first century, one of the most important events for Orthodoxy worldwide was the Holy and Great Council of the Orthodox Church, held in Crete in June 2016.

This book does not claim to cover everything there is to know about the Orthodox Church. Its much more modest aim is to open a window into a faith that is all too often unfamiliar. Readers will discover the basic outlines of the history and the unique theology and worship of Eastern Christianity. The history of Christianity is complex, and Christianity itself is multifaceted. Orthodoxy offers a different understanding of the nature of the Church, its Eastern reality, its pastoral concerns, and its relationship to the sacred and to the arts.

PART 1
The History of the Orthodox Church

Chapter 1
The Early Church

IN THIS CHAPTER

- The first Christian communities
- The time of persecutions
- The Constantinian era

The history of Orthodoxy is an integral part of the broader history of Christianity. The story begins in the Middle East with Jesus Christ, who founded the Church when he gathered his twelve disciples.

Orthodoxy shares these roots with all other Christian traditions because during the first centuries of Christianity, there were not yet separate Churches, but only one undivided Church.The first millennium was not only a formative period. It also constitutes the original Christian experience to which Orthodoxy is connected through the apostolic continuity of the early Christian communities.

| The first Christian communities

The very first Christian communities were concentrated in Jerusalem. Their teachings were based essentially on the eyewitness testimony of the Apostles, Christ's disciples, after the Holy Spirit descended on them on Pentecost (Acts 2:2-4). Men and women alike heard their preaching and began to be baptized, receiving the name of Christians (Acts 11:26) as members of the Church. Christians scattered throughout the Mediterranean basin, some driven by missionary zeal and others fleeing persecution by the Roman authorities. New local communities were formed. These communities were the Churches to which the Apostle Paul referred as "the church of God in [location of the community]" Rome, Corinth, and Thessalonica. It was within these communities that the memory of the life and teachings of Christ, his miracles, and the events of his passion, resurrection, and ascension were preserved.

| Life in the first Christian communities

These early communities were soon faced with a major question: how should pagan converts be received into the Church? As soon as Christianity spread beyond Jerusalem, it began to attract converts from paganism and not only Judaism, from which it originated. A disagreement arose between those who believed that the Law of Moses should be imposed on non-Jewish Christian converts and those who held that faith in Christ alone was enough for membership in the Church. An assembly, or council, was held in Jerusalem to determine which practice to follow. The Apostles chose the second option (Acts 15:5-29). This central event not only defined the collegial way in which the Church would function, according to the Orthodox interpretation, but also unleashed its missionary energy. The spread of Christianity was a direct response to one of Christ's commandments: "Go therefore and make disciples of all nations, baptizing them in the name of the Father and of the Son and of the Holy Spirit" (Matthew 28:19).[1]

---

[1] All quotations from the Bible are taken from the New Revised Standard Version, Updated Edition, National Council of the Churches of Christ, 2021.

The journeys of the Apostles, particularly the Apostle Paul, a Jew who converted to Christianity after experiencing a vision on the road to Damascus (Acts 9:3-19), led to the establishment of Christian communities in the main centers of the Roman Empire and sometimes even beyond its borders. As Christianity encountered Roman culture and the great cities of the Empire, the first ecclesiastical administrative structures began to emerge, although their functions and responsibilities were not yet fully defined. As these early communities formed in urban centers and the surrounding countryside, they organized themselves on a local level around their bishops, who were assisted by priests and deacons.

Jerusalem

A holy city for all three monotheistic religions (Judaism, Christianity, and Islam), Jerusalem is the birthplace of Christianity. It quickly became a pilgrimage destination for all Christians. Today, the Church of the Holy Sepulcher, where both the site of the crucifixion (Golgotha) and the Resurrection Grotto are located, is administered by three Christian denominations: the Greek Orthodox Patriarchate of Jerusalem, the Roman Catholic Church, and the Armenian Apostolic Church.

The central place of Scripture and the liturgy

Thanks to ancient writings which date back to the first century AD, we know that early Christian communities were centered around a worship service that the Orthodox Church still calls the Divine Liturgy (work of the people) or Eucharist. The early Christian community structure was based on three roles: bishops, priests, and deacons. These roles were closely linked to the liturgical prayers that shaped the life and organization of these first assemblies and connected to one another by the sacramental presence of Christ in the bread and wine of the Eucharist. The Last Supper, or Mystical Supper as it is usually called in Orthodoxy, is the foundation of the understanding of the Church as the body of Christ (Matthew 26:26-29 and 1 Corinthians 12:27). Christ's words during this meal define the core of Christianity:

> *I give you a new commandment, that you love one another. Just as I have loved you, you also should love one another. By this everyone will know that you are my disciples, if you have love for one another.*
> John 13:34-35

In the decades following the resurrection, the oral preaching of the apostles was gradually written down. These ancient texts, which were collected with the aim of passing on the truth of the Christian experience based on the revelation of Jesus Christ as God, form the New Testament, or Gospel. The Greek word for Gospel, *"evangelio,"* literally means "good news." The familiar English word Gospel means the same thing: it is derived from the literal translation of *"evangelio"* into Old English as *"god spel."* The twenty-seven books of the New Testament existed alongside other documents in the early years of the Church. Most of these documents are considered apocryphal (hidden), since they originated among gnostic-leaning or even heretical groups and were not included in the canonical Bible. Some were even condemned in strong terms by the Church. Others, however, like the *Protoevangelion of James* or other apocryphal writings, which describes the youth of the Virgin Mary and Christ, provided tremendous inspiration for the iconography and hymns that are still used by the Orthodox Church today.

The books of the New Testament

- The Four Gospels (Matthew, Mark, Luke, and John)
- The Acts of the Apostles
- Fourteen Epistles of Paul
- Two Epistles of Peter
- Three Epistles of John
- One Epistle of James
- One Epistle of Jude
- Revelation

The Apostolic Writings

From the earliest times, every Christian community celebrated the Eucharist on Sunday, in memory of Christ's resurrection. This principle of worship remains profoundly anchored in the Orthodox Church. Unity is guaranteed by mutual recognition among bishops, forming a communion of Churches. This principle, which was the bedrock of the identity of the first Christian communities, appeared as early as the writings of the direct heirs of the apostles. Known as the writings of the Apostolic Fathers, these documents from the first and second centuries AD represent the first Greek-language Christian literature. They include the two epistles of Clement of Rome, the letter of Polycarp of Smyrna, *The Pastor of Hermas*, and the *Didache* (also known as *The Lord's Teaching Through the Twelve Apostles to the Nations*) and are the key sources for studies of this period, since they are a direct expression of the reality of early Christianity.

The time of persecutions

Challenges to the religious and sociopolitical order

Christianity was persecuted by the Roman Empire throughout its first three centuries. Imperial oppression increased as Christianity became increasingly distinct from Judaism, a split that became irreversible with the destruction of the Temple in Jerusalem in 70 AD. Six years earlier, Christians had been accused of setting the great fire of Rome by the Emperor Nero (54-68),[2] who systematically attacked them as enemies of the empire. Numerous historical sources from the period detail the accusations leveled at Christians. In 106, for example, the Emperor Trajan (98-117) ordered that offerings be made to the pagan gods following a major military victory. When St. Ignatius of Antioch (c. 108/140) refused to comply, he was imprisoned and then sent to Rome to be fed to the lions the next year. On his road to martyrdom, Ignatius left behind an extensive correspondence.

---

2 For historical figures who held a position such as emperor, patriarch, or pope, their dates of office are given in parentheses. For other figures, including theologians and philosophers, the dates given are those of their birth and death.

Despite their intensity, these periods of persecution were sporadic. In the second century, Trajan (98-117) was a fierce opponent of Christianity, as was Marcus Aurelius (161-180), who authorized the use of torture to induce Christians to deny their faith and had them systematically hunted down. In the following century, Decius (249-251) aimed to stamp out Christianity, while three decades later, Diocletian (284-305) destroyed churches and stripped Christians of their rights, having them tortured and imprisoned before condeming them to death.

These periods of persecution occured for several reasons. Romans viewed Christianity as a secret society, and the subject of highly lurid rumors. The first Christian communities sought to preserve the sanctity of their worship by only gradually revealing their practices and beliefs to new converts through a progressive process of initiation. This secrecy inspired false accusations of a vast array of horrible practices, including cannibalism. No less serious to the Roman mind was that when Christians refused to sacrifice to the Roman gods or worship the emperor, they were defying the established social and religious field.

The Roman persecutions ended in 313 with the Edict of Milan.

| Defending Christianity through literature

The times of persecution profoundly influenced early Christianity as well as Orthodoxy today, particularly through the veneration of the martyrs and the dense literature written to defend Christianity, known as apologetics, produced during this period.

The apologetic literature of the first three centuries covers several major themes.

- Powerful arguments against Gnosticism, which was considered a heresy contrary to emerging Christian doctrine. Saint Irenaeus of Lyon, who was martyred in 202, was particularly active in this vein.

- An educational dimension, which brought the Christian faith into contact with Greek philosophy. This strand is perhaps best represented by Origen (ca. 185-ca. 254), the greatest author of the Christian East. Origen's work explores a profound question: how can we interpret the Scriptures and go beyond a literal reading to discover their symbolic and allegorical meaning? Origen's influence on the later development of Christian doctrine is undeniable. He is, however, a highly controversial figure due to some of his more questionable positions like the the pre-existence of souls.

- Debates about how those who had denied Christ should be received back into the Church following the waves of persecution. This question sparked serious tensions between two opposing camps. The rigorists, represented by Tertullian (160-220) – the first Christian author to write in Latin instead of Greek, the language of the New Testament and the dominant language of early Christianity – rejected the acceptance of repentant apostates. Their opponents, including Saint Cyprian of Carthage (200-250), took a more nuanced, pastoral approach. Saint Cyprian argued that apostates should be allowed to return to the Church under certain conditions, following an appropriate period of penitence. This debate profoundly influenced the Latin Christian literature of the period, with its focus on the importance of unity within communities at a time when they were riven by theological and pastoral tensions.

The Constantinian era

The end of the persecutions

When Constantine the Great (306-337) rose to power, Christianity finally entered smoother waters. The long period of persecutions officially ended in 313 when Constantine promulgated the Edict of Milan, which decreed religious tolerance under which "no one whatsoever should be denied the opportunity to give his heart to the observance of the Christian religion, or of that religion which he should think best for himself." This change occurred after a famous episode in the emperor's life. As he was marching through Gaul (present day France) with his army, Constantine saw a luminous cross in the sky, emblazoned with the words "in this sign, conquer." Despite this experience, Constantine was baptized only as he was dying. In the decades that followed, Christianity gradually replaced paganism throughout the Roman Empire, eventually leading to the emergence of a Christian Roman Empire, which enabled Christianity to grow throughout the known world.

The Church of the catacombs becomes an imperial Church

The emperor's commitment to favoring Christianity over other religions was a determining factor in its rising influence. A few decades after Constantine, the emperor Theodosius (379-395) would officially reject paganism and recognize Christianity as the state religion.

One direct consequence of the drastic change in the Roman Empire's official religious policy was the transfer of the capital from Rome to Constantinople (now Istanbul, Türkiye) in 324. As is often the case, the move was driven by a combination of political, economic, and religious factors. On the religious side, Constantine's aim was to build a new capital, free of pagan symbols, for the creation of a future Christian empire. The new capital of the Roman Empire would have a crucial influence on the development of Orthodoxy.

> **Constantinople**
>
> *Built on the site of an ancient Greek city called Byzantium, the city to which Constantine gave his name became the political center of the Eastern Roman Empire. Known as the "New Rome" from the fifth century on, or simply as "the City," it was the political heart of what would become the Byzantine Empire, epitomized by the magnificent sixth century cathedral of Hagia Sophia. Over the centuries that followed, the growth of Islam gradually sapped Byzantine political power. Constantinople was besieged several times before falling for the first time to the Latins during the Fourth*

> Crusade in 1204. It ultimately fell to the Ottomans on May 29, 1453. It was not until 1928, however, that Constantinople was officially renamed Istanbul. Today, the city's many churches and other Byzantine sites stand alongside Ottoman monuments, making it a unique crossroads of East and West. Constantinople still remains the seat of the Ecumenical Patriarchate, the first among equals of Orthodox Churches.

| The development of Christian doctrine and the councils

The shift in the empire's religious policy also affected the development of Christian doctrine. Constantine wanted to put an end to the theological controversies that divided Christians and unify the Christian faith at a time when it was becoming the heart of Roman society. With these aims in mind, he convened the first ecumenical council in Nicaea, near Constantinople in 325. The Council brought together hundreds of bishops, whose task was to reach an agreement on the nature of Christ and refute the teachings of Arius. It also offered them an opportunity to explore the relationship between the revelation of the Christian faith and Greek philosophy in greater depth. The creed produced by the council initiated a unification of Christianity, which was key to the emperor's political goals. For the emperor, meanwhile, the unity of the faith should advance the unity of the empire. While other local councils had already been held, this was the first council on an Empire-wide scale. The council of Nicaea was to be the first of a series of seven councils, known as ecumenical (œcuméné, "the inhabited world") councils due to their authority, which would define the key principles of the Christian faith. The fourth century marked the beginning of the golden age of Christian theology, art, and culture.

| Key points

- Orthodoxy originated with the birth of Christianity. The early Christian era was marked by a formative period and the transmission of Christ's teachings. Over time, the Church developed both its doctrine and an ecclesiastical structure rooted in worship.

- As Christianity spread throughout the Mediterranean basin, the first Christian literature appeared. It was based on the transmission of Christ's words, with the compilation of the New Testament. Later writings by the Apostolic Fathers and the Apologists expressed tremendous teaching and missionary energy.

- This growth occurred in the extremely unfavorable context of a Roman Empire that remained committed to paganism. The time of persecutions ended in the fourth century with the accession of the Emperor Constantine, who gave Christianity an ever-increasing role in the empire. The growth of Christianity was marked by three key steps: the Edict of Milan, the founding of Constantinople, and the Council of Nicaea.

Chapter 2

Unity in the Byzantine Empire, Division Among Christians

IN THIS CHAPTER

- Christianity in the Byzantine Empire
- The Oriental Orthodox Churches
- The Schism of 1054

Orthodoxy is often viewed as the Eastern fringe of Christianity, an understandable perspective given its presence in the Middle East and Mediterranean. On a historical level, its development throughout the Byzantine period enabled an encounter between Hellenistic culture and philosophy and the principles of the Gospel. The Roman Empire officially adopted Christianity in the fourth century, making it essential to clearly define the content of Christian teaching. The decisions of local and ecumenical councils and the teachings of the Church Fathers formed a religious synthesis of Jewish and Greek culture. During the same period, the emergence of monasticism, particularly in the deserts of Egypt and Palestine, gave these theological ideas an experiential, embodied form. Orthodox theology is not intended as a purely speculative exercise. Asceticism inspires contemplation of God and theology is to the intellect what prayer is to the heart: grace.[3]

Christianity in the Byzantine Empire

A principle of imperial unity

In the fourth century, Christianity gradually replaced paganism and was eventually made the official imperial religion by Emperor Theodosius (379-395). From that point on, Christianity played a essential role in the Eastern Roman Empire, which was entirely Christianized by the time of Justinian (527-565). The boundaries of ecclesiastical jurisdictions coincided with the empire's administrative borders. For the political authorities, the goal was not simply to adopt a new religion but, as Fr. John Meyendorff has astutely observed, to make the Christian faith a principle of imperial unity.[4]

During this period, the unity of the Empire was threatened by doctrinal conflicts, heresies, and disagreements about the faith. In order to resolve these disputes, successive emperors convened a series of councils. The church of Rome was represented at these councils and accepted their decisions since it had not yet broken with Constantinople. The Orthodox Church recognizes seven ecumenical councils, from the first council held in Nicaea in 325 under Constantine to what is generally viewed as the last, the seventh, also held in Nicaea in 787, which authorized the use of icons, or sacred images, in churches.

---

3 This ascetic theology was also extensively taught in the Persian Gulf region by Isaac the Syrian in the mid-sixth century. See: *Isaac the Syrian, The Ascetical Homilies of Saint Isaac the Syrian* (Holy Transfiguration Monastery, 2011)
4 Meyendorff, John, *Imperial Unity and Christian Divisions* (St. Vladimir's Seminary Press, 2011).

> **Seven Ecumenical Councils**[5]
>
> 1. **Nicaea I**, *325:* the Son is of the same substance as the Father. He is "consubstantial" with the Father. The council condemned Arianism.
> 2. **Constantinople I, 381:** the Holy Spirit is fully God.
> 3. **Ephesus, 431:** Mary is known as the Mother of God (Theotokos). She gave birth to the second person of the Trinity.
> 4. **Chalcedon, 451:** Jesus is fully human and fully divine.
> 5. **Constantinople II, 553**: the three persons of the Trinity are consubstantial. The council rejected all doctrines that define Christ as two persons, or hypostases. It confirmed the orthodoxy of the teachings of Saint Cyril of Alexandria and condemned his adversaries.
> 6. **Constantinople III, 680-681:** Jesus Christ has two wills, one divine and one human, inseparably united in one person. The council condemned monothelitism.
> 7. **Nicaea II, 787**: the holy images (icons) of Christ, the Mother of God, and the saints rightfully belong in churches and may be venerated.

These seven ecumenical councils, which were central to the development of the Orthodox dogmatic tradition, served a dual purpose: clarifying the definition of Christ's identity for the Church as true God and true man and reinforcing social and political cohesion. Doctrine became both a religious and a political issue. Despite possible political intrigue, faith is not an ideology but a central question in understanding the mystery of salvation.

During this period, the relationship between Church and State was theorized by the Emperor Justinian, who described it using the term "symphony" in his Novella 6, promulgated in 535:

> *The greatest gifts given by God to men by His supreme kindness are the priesthood and the empire, of which the first serves the things of*

---

[5] The Council *in Trullo,* or *Quinisext* Council (692), shares the authority of the Sixth Ecumenical Council of Constantinople III. It focused on canonical discipline rather than the definition of the faith.

God and the second rules the things of men and assumes the burden of care for them. Both proceed from one source and adorn the life of man.

It was also Justinian who ordered the construction of Hagia Sophia cathedral in the imperial capital.

> **Hagia Sophia, Holy Wisdom**
>
> *This monumental basilica in the heart of Istanbul (Türkiye) is dedicated to the wisdom (sophia) of God. An Orthodox church until 1453, it was the center of Orthodox Christianity for nearly a thousand years and was the largest cathedral in the world until the construction of Saint Peter's Basilica in Rome. Today, it is the greatest surviving example of Byzantine architecture. The current structure was built by the Emperor Justinian in the sixth century. It was turned into a mosque in 1453 before becoming a museum in 1935 and then once again a mosque in 2020.*

From synthesis to schism

In the East, a synthesis of spirituality and dogma developed between the fourth and eighth centuries, with the monastic experience of the Desert Fathers (Evagrius, Macarius and John Climacus) and the formalization of doctrine by the Church Fathers (Basil the Great, Gregory the Theologian, John Chrysostom, Dionysius the Areopagite, Maximus the Confessor, and John of Damascus). In the ninth century, the Eastern church began to build on this foundation to develop a topic that the Patriarch of Constantinople Photius the Great debated with the Carolingians: a theology of the Holy Spirit. This theology of the Holy Spirit was based on the contemplative movement known as *hesychasm* (Greek for "peace," "silence," and "prayer") which teaches the vision of God and the deification of the human person.

> **The Desert Fathers**
>
> *The Desert Fathers were mostly monks living in Egypt and Syria in the fourth and fifth centuries. They produced a rich spiritual literature that bears witness to the beginnings of monasticism. In addition to a few treatises, their teachings have been preserved in the form of anecdotes, precepts, and sayings known as* apophthegmata.

The centuries that followed were marked by the schism between Eastern and Western Christianity (1054) and the gradual decline of Byzantium, which was precipitated by the Fourth Crusade in 1204, when the Latins conquered Constantinople and held it for sixty years. In the eleventh century, Simeon the New Theologian defended a purely charismatic idea of the Church. In the fourteenth century, Gregory Palamas, a monk on Mount Athos, affirmed that, contrary to the Latin scholastic thought of the time, grace is uncreated and that is a distinction between God's energies, in which we can participate, and His essence, in which we cannot. The Orthodox Church accepted these teachings as canonical during later councils.

The Eastern Roman Empire finally fell when Constantinople was taken by Mehmet II on May 29, 1453. To continue to trace the development of the Orthodox world after that point, we will need to turn our attention to the Slavic countries of Eastern Europe. But before the Great Schism of the eleventh century, a first split with the Oriental Orthodox Churches had already taken place.

The Oriental Orthodox Churches

Antioch vs. Alexandria

In the fifth century, the Christians on the southeastern fringes of the Roman Empire broke away from the Orthodox mainstream. Christians in the region formed a mosaic of different communities whose tremendous vitality would leave an imprint on later Arab and Muslim culture. The history of the Oriental Orthodox Churches can be traced back to the first Christian communities in Jerusalem and the Mediterranean basin, the direct heirs of the Apostles and their successors–a common past shared with the undivided Church.

They split from the Orthodox Church came over the question of "who is Christ" in the wake of the Ecumenical Councils of the fifth century, particularly the Council of Chalcedon in 451. The Oriental Orthodox Churches are also known as the "pre-," "anti-," and "non-Chalcedonian" churches. However, "Oriental Orthodox" is the most neutral and most commonly used term and is distinct from the "Eastern" Orthodox Church.

The major debates during the first centuries of Christianity were conditioned by the opposition between two schools of biblical interpretation: the more literal school of Antioch and the more allegorical school of Alexandria.

This division, which still persists today, is reflected in the two different groups of Oriental Orthodox Churches.

- The Assyrian Church, sometimes pejoratively referred to as "Nestorian," is inspired by the Antiochian school. It focuses on the humanity of Jesus and rejects the third Ecumenical Council (Ephesus, 431). It is present in Persia and Mesopotamia and reached its apogee in the eighth and ninth centuries under Abbasid domination. Assyrian missionaries traveled as far as China and Tibet before the Mongol invasions forced them back starting in the thirteenth century.

- The Armenian, Syriac, Coptic, Ethiopian, and Indian Malankara Churches are sometimes referred to as "Monophysite." These churches, which are inspired by the Alexandrian school, emphasize Christ's divinity and reject the fourth Ecumenical Council (Chalcedon, 451). As they were isolated by the emergence of Islam, with the exception of the Armenian Church, they formed separate national entities.

These Churches, which call themselves Orthodox, are in fact very similar to the Eastern Orthodox Church in their structure, mindset, and religious practices. Their existence shows a Semitic ressourcement, particularly with the increasing use of the Syriac language in late antiquity. Syriac, which grew out of the Aramaic spoken in the Assyrian and Achaemenid Empires and is the ancestor of modern Hebrew and Arabic, developed in the schools of Edessa and Nisibis. Syriac culture reached its full flowering under Islamic domination with extensive translation activities, particularly of scientific and philosophical texts, that made it a major player in the intellectual and cultural effervescence of the eighth and ninth centuries.

The Oriental Orthodox Churches have sustained a strong sense of their own history and tradition through their very active monastic tradition. However, their position as minorities and their fragmentation have left them extremely vulnerable both to persecution and to Catholic and Protestant missionary efforts. Despite their vulnerability, they remain an essential part of the religious make-up of the Middle East.

Today, there are some 60 million Oriental Orthodox Christians worldwide. The majority live in Ethiopia, Egypt, Eritrea, Armenia, India, Syria, and Lebanon, although there are also large diaspora communities in Asia, Europe (mainly Western Europe), the Americas, and Australia. In the United States, these groups are organized within the Standing Conference of Oriental Orthodox Churches.

The Eastern Rite Catholic Churches

The Eastern Churches also include the Eastern Rite Catholic Churches, sometimes derogatorily referred to as "Uniate" Churches, communities in Eastern Europe and the Middle East which Rome detached from the Orthodox Church by military force or political influence in the years after 1453. This Roman strategy was based on two medieval attempts at reunification: the Council of Lyon in 1274 and the Council of Florence in 1438-1439. Today, the Eastern Rite Catholic Churches include the Chaldean Catholic Church, which originated in Oriental Orthodoxy and now outnumbers the Assyrian Church from which it sprang. Other Eastern Catholic groups came from Orthodoxy, including the Greek Catholic Ukrainians, whose identity was reinforced by persecution under Stalin, and the Melkites, whose Arabic culture is blended with theological nostalgia for Byzantium.

Only the Maronites, descendants of Syriac and Monophysite clans in Syria who had taken refuge in the mountains of Lebanon and submitted to Roman authority during the Crusades, have no

Orthodox counterpart. Since the Balamand (Lebanon) Agreement, signed by the Catholic and Orthodox Churches in 1993, "Uniatism" has been explicitly rejected as a model of unity.

> **The fate of Christians in the Middle East**
>
> *The depredations of ISIS and the Syrian civil war have left Middle Eastern Christians in a perilous position. This mosaic of Catholic, Eastern Orthodox, Oriental Orthodox, and Protestant communities in the Middle East, particularly Iraq, Syria, Israel, Lebanon, and Egypt, forms a living link with the first Christians. As a minority, they are particularly vulnerable to the region's bloody conflicts. Their forced exile is an unprecedented break with the past in the very birthplace of Christianity.*
>
> *As French historian and theologian Jean-François Colosimo has demonstrated, Middle Eastern Christians play a key role as mediators between East and West and in the Muslim-majority environment of the Middle East: "Christians live out their vocation as a third party that is essential for the emancipation of all, including their Muslim compatriots."*[6]

| The Schism of 1054

| A political, cultural, and theological split

1054 is generally accepted as the date of the break between the Churches of Constantinople and Rome. While it is largely symbolic, this date represents the consummation of a progressive estrangement between the "two lungs" of the Roman Empire–one final step in the long process of fracture which continued into later centuries. The crisis which led to the schism was as much political and cultural as it was theological. The main theological point of contention between East and West was the use of the expression *Filioque* (and of the Son) in the Nicene Creed.

---

6 Colosimo, Jean-François, *Les Hommes en trop. La malédiction des chrétiens d'Orient* (Paris: Fayard, 2014).

Long before the crisis erupted, however, Eastern and Western Christianity had already lost their ability to understand each other as the unity of the Mediterranean world gradually vanished. The founding of Constantinople did nothing to help matters. The barbarian invasions of the fifth century had left the Western Empire permanently weakened, while the East was hard hit by invaders from the north and east. The growing estrangement between East and West was worsened by the iconoclastic controversy. Rome, which was weak and vulnerable, turned to the Frankish Kingdom rather than to Byzantium for protection. In 800, the Frankish king Charlemagne (742-814) was crowned emperor by Pope Leo III (747-816). The creation of the Holy Roman Empire in the West received a chilly response from the Byzantine Empire, which viewed it as a challenge to imperial unity.

Language was another factor in the estrangement of East and West. While both halves of the Roman world shared a common classical heritage and the Greek language remained in widespread use among intellectuals in the West as late as the fifth century, by the sixth century few Greeks spoke Latin and few Latins spoke Greek.

As the political situation grew increasingly tense and the cultural commonalities between East and West vanished, the break soon spread to church affairs. The two Churches developed different forms of administration. According to Metropolitan Kallistos (Ware) of Diokleia,

> *The western Church became centralized to a degree unknown anywhere in the four Patriarchates of the east (except possibly in Egypt). Monarchy in the west; in the east collegiality.*[7]

| Two divergences

The estrangement between East and West continued to deepen. There were two major divergences between them: the universal claims of the Papacy and the question of the *Filioque*, which ultimately catalyzed the schism. The *Filioque* dispute focused on the

---

[7] Ware, Kallistos *The Orthodox Church* (Third edition published in Penguin Books, 2015).

Creed of Nicaea-Constantinople (325-381), and more specifically on the article on the Holy Spirit:

> I believe... In the Holy Spirit, the giver of life, who proceeds from the Father [and the son, (Filioque)], and who together with the Father and Son is worshiped and glorified.

The introduction of the words "and the Son," which probably originated in Toledo (Spain) in the sixth century, spread throughout the Western Church and became official doctrine under Charlemagne. He was the first to make it a topic of controversy with the East, accusing the Byzantines of heresy for their refusal to adopt it. The Byzantine response to Charlemagne's accusations did not come until 850 – and when it did, it was a rejection of the addition as an alteration of the common faith of the Church. Today, the Orthodox Church still considers this modification theologically incorrect and believes that the Holy Spirit proceeds only from the Father. To believe otherwise would undermine the Holy Spirit's dignity and equality with the other persons of the Holy Trinity.

In addition to these real theological concerns, the *Filioque* debate played on the perception of differences in the relationship between East and West. All differences were now seen as harmful to unity.

Romans and Byzantines, who had already come into conflict in the mission field of Slavic Eastern Europe in the ninth century, clashed again over the *Filioque*. Pope Nicholas I (858-867), who hoped to expand his political hegemony eastward, rejected the advances of the envoys sent by the Patriarch of Constantinople Photius I (858-867 and 877-886). The conflict between the two halves of the Christian world escalated through the tenth century and the first half of the eleventh century. The *Filioque* dispute broke out once again in the mid-eleventh century, against the backdrop of ecclesiastical power struggles and conflicts over liturgical practices such as the use of unleavened bread in the Italian Byzantine dependencies – and this time, there would be no path to reconciliation. In 1053-1054, Pope Leo IX (1049-1054) was invited to Constantinople by the Patriarch Michael Cerularius (1000-1059). The Pope sent three Roman legates to represent him. However, their meetings soon disintegrated, with each side's arguments falling on deaf ears. The papal legates ultimately ended this final attempt at dialogue by placing a bull of excommunication on the altar of Hagia Sophia, accusing the Byzantines of removing the *Filioque* from the creed among other alleged misdeeds. While various attempts at reunification were made in the following centuries, the schism effectively terminated the relationship between East and West. It became final when Constantinople fell to the Crusaders in 1204.

> **Differences between Orthodoxy and Catholicism**
>
> ***Filioque***
> *The Orthodox Church confesses that the "Holy Spirit proceeds from the Father" (cf. John 15:26). According to Orthodox teaching, the fact that the West changed the wording to "from the Father and the Son (Filioque)" diminishes the dignity of the person of the Holy Spirit.*
>
> ***Catholicity***
> *In the wording of the Creed of Nicaea-Constantinople (325-381), the Orthodox Church proclaims that it is "catholic," although not in the sense of geographical universality adopted later by the Church of Rome. Beginning in the tenth century, the Papacy laid claim to divinely ordered universal jurisdiction. Rome came to believe that its jurisdictional power extended to the East, after waves of barbarian invasions had left it the primary consolidating force in a fragmented West. This meant a change in the nature of Rome's primacy. The Orthodox Church, which recognizes what it considers Rome's traditional primacy of honor, does not accept the transformation of that primacy into universal supremacy.[8]*
>
> ***Papal infallibility***
> *The doctrine of papal infallibility, which was proclaimed by the First Vatican Council in 1870, is unacceptable to the Orthodox Church. Orthodoxy emphasizes that the people of God are the depositary of the truth of the Church.*

---

8 For an Orthodox perspective on Roman primacy, see the excellent work by Clément, Olivier, *You are Peter: an Orthodox Theologian's Reflection on the Papal Primacy* (New City Press, 2003).

> **Immaculate Conception**
> Mary was recognized as the "Mother of God" by the Ecumenical Council of Ephesus in 431 and as "ever-virgin" by the Council of Constantinople in 553. In 1884, Rome added to that list, proclaiming her "exempt from original sin." However, the Latin doctrine of original sin is not found in the writings of the Greek Fathers, who rejected any idea of inherited ontological guilt. According to Orthodox teaching, human nature inherited the corruption that followed Adam's sin and fall, not guilt for Adam's sin, because sin is always a personal act.

| Key points

- The history of Orthodoxy is anchored in the East. It is often treated as synonymous with Byzantium, but is actually far broader. However, the history of the Eastern Roman Empire and of Christianity in the imperial capital of Constantinople does mark a decisive step in the baptism of cultures. Fr. Georges Florovsky refers to this process as the "Christianization of Hellenism."

- This movement was marred by division and theological disagreements. In the theological and political context of the fifth century, the unity of the Byzantine Empire led to the first great schism within Christianity, the break with the Oriental Orthodox Churches.

- Divisions between Christians increased with the schism between the Eastern and Western Churches in 1054. Theology became enmeshed with politics. The clash between two different visions of Christianity made this estrangement permanent.

Chapter 3

From the Fall of Constantinople to Today

> **IN THIS CHAPTER**
>
> - The challenges of Muslim domination
> - The rise of Slavic Orthodoxy
> - The Orthodox diaspora

The fall of Constantinople and the Byzantine Empire radically changed the history of Orthodoxy. The center of gravity of the Orthodox world shifted northwards as the Churches that found themselves under Ottoman domination sought above all to survive in their new position as minorities. In the Slavic world, the growing social and political importance of the Orthodox Church and the rise of Russia, which became an empire in the sixteenth century, led to a readjustment of the balance of power between the spiritual and temporal authorities.

The challenges of Muslim domination

Constantinople fell to Sultan Mehmet II on May 29, 1453, the date that traditionally marks the fall of the Byzantine Empire. As many authors, most notably Steven Runciman, have observed, after the fall of the empire, Byzantine civilization began its second life within Orthodoxy. Is Orthodoxy really the heir of Byzantium? Even today, the Orthodox Churches remain profoundly influenced by the Byzantines' cultural expression, their relationship to art, and even their understanding of politics.

The fall of Constantinople

The fall of the Eastern Roman Empire put an end to a dream that had lasted over a thousand years. Sultan Mehmet II (1444-1446 and 1451-1481) conquered the city of Constantinople, upending the lives of its Christian inhabitants and Orthodoxy more broadly. However, the conqueror had no intention of wiping out Christianity in the Ottoman Empire. In fact, he personally installed the new Patriarch of Constantinople, Gennadios Scholarios (1454-1456, 1462-1463, and 1464-1465). Gennadios was known for his opposition to the Church of Rome, dashing the hopes of those who wanted to see the Union of Ferrara-Florence become a reality (1438-1439). This move enabled the new sultan to ensure his subjects' loyalty. However, Orthodox Christians found themselves relegated to life as second-class citizens in their own homelands. Hagia Sophia, the crown jewel of Orthodoxy, became a mosque. The fall of Constantinople triggered a slow social death-spiral that was accompanied by serious moral and intellectual decay in the church hierarchy. Corruption and simony – the sale of religious offices – were widespread among the clergy. Church positions were sold for money, while newly elected Patriarchs had to promise huge sums of money to persuade the sultan to produce the authorization (*berat*) required for their enthronement.

Since the Ottoman Empire was constantly at war, and therefore constantly in need of money, intrigue within the Church and outside pressures led to the frequent replacement of the Patriarch. The same bishop might be made patriarch several times.

Ottoman domination required Christian clergy to submit to the Muslim power of the Sublime Porte. Christian communities, which had become minorities, were organized as an independent ethno-religious group within the Empire, called the "Roman Nation" (*rum millet*). The community's organization was based on the structure of the church, and the Ecumenical Patriarch of Constantinople was not only a spiritual but also a civil leader, later referred to as an *ethnarch*. This system survived into the twentieth century and traces of it persisted as late as 1959, when Archbishop Makarios III (1950-1977) was elected as the first president of the Republic of Cyprus.

| Autocephaly

During the Ottoman period, the Ecumenical Patriarchate of Constantinople remained a powerful core of Orthodoxy. The other Patriarchates of the Empire – Alexandria, Antioch, and Jerusalem, and later the Churches of Romania, Serbia, and Bulgaria – were under its authority. The Ecumenical Patriarchate lost that authority in the wake of the revolutions that led to the creation of new nation-states in the Balkans as the Ottoman Empire broke apart before becoming the modern Türkiye in 1923 under the leadership of Mustafa Kemal Atatürk (1881-1938). As these new states emerged, their national Churches organized and became independent of the Ecumenical Patriarchate:

- Church of Greece, organized in 1833 after the Greek Revolution of 1821, recognized by the Ecumenical Patriarchate in 1850;
- Church of Romania, organized in 1864, recognized in 1885;
- Church of Bulgaria, re-established in 1871, recognized in 1945;
- Church of Serbia, re-established and recognized in 1879.

The recognition of the Church of Bulgaria took longer than the others due to a dispute with the Ecumenical Patriarchate. That dispute led to the 1872 Council of Constantinople, which officially condemned all forms of ecclesiastical racism (ethnophyletism).

The confessional period

The Ottoman period also had a major impact on the development of Orthodox theology, which was torn between rigid traditionalism and westernization. During this period, Orthodox scholars traveled to the great universities of Italy, Germany, England, and France and Orthodox theology was transformed by the influence of Catholicism and Protestantism. The Orthodox theologian Fr. Georges Florovsky (1893-1979) referred to this process as a pseudomorphosis, a westernization of Orthodox thought, to which traditionalist movements like the nineteenth century Russian Slavophiles reacted. The echoes of this period still reverberate today.

The diplomatic influence wielded by Western embassies, Catholic and Protestant alike, in their interactions with the Orthodox population of Constantinople was accompanied by intense missionary efforts to convert Eastern Christians. In 1573, against the backdrop of the religious wars of the sixteenth century, when there were hopes of a potential alliance between Orthodox and Protestants, Orthodoxy began its first dialog with the Protestant world. The dialogue lasted about a decade before Ecumenical Patriarch Jeremiah II, known as *Tranos*, (1572-1579, 1580-1584, and 1587-1595) put an end to it. He felt that Protestantism was too distant from Orthodox theological positions, particularly on the questions of free will, grace, the sacraments, and the veneration of saints.

In the Slavic world, meanwhile, the Orthodox population in the Kingdom of Poland-Lithuania, which extended into modern-day Ukraine, lived under the rule of a Catholic sovereign. In 1596, at the Council of Brest-Litovsk, the local Orthodox hierarchy decided to submit to Rome. These hierarchs adopted the principles of the Council of Florence (1438-1439), which meant recognizing papal supremacy while maintaining their own traditional liturgical practices (the possibility of married clergy, the Byzantine-rite liturgy, etc.). The council of 1596 polarized the opposition between Catholics and Orthodox, an antagonism that persists today in a milder form.

From the sixteenth century onwards, Orthodoxy was heavily influenced by outside political and theological forces. Saint Cyril Lucaris (1572-1638) embodied the trends of the era. Because Lucaris was profoundly anti-Roman, he cultivated relationships with Protestant chancelleries with the goal of limiting Catholic influence in the Ottoman Empire. His proximity to the Protestant world was not only political but also theological. The Confession that he published in Geneva in 1629 clearly reflected distinctly Calvinist positions. A few years later, two local councils rejected Lucaris' teachings. However, that did not keep him from becoming the Ecumenical Patriarch of Constantinople at least five times.

In response to Lucaris' Confession, two other Orthodox hierarchs hastily developed their own counter-confessions. Petro Mohyla (1596-1646), the Orthodox Metropolitan of Kyiv, directly based his work on Latin theology manuals. Several decades later, Dositheos II, Patriarch of Jerusalem (1669-1707), was also inspired by Roman Catholic theology. His writings were approved by the Council of Jerusalem of 1672. One of the key characteristics of this influence was the use of the concept of *transubstantiation*,[9] borrowed directly from the scholastic distinction between substance and accident.

Despite these influences, this period also saw profound theological developments that directly contributed to a revival of the faith. Hesychasm played a crucial role in this movement which, in the eighteenth century, took on the name of the *kollyvades* controversy on Mount Athos. The movement took its name from the *kollyva* (boiled wheat) used during memorial services. Its advocates were Athonite monks who strictly followed holy tradition. They maintained that memorial services should not be conducted on Sundays, the day of the Lord's Resurrection, but rather on Saturday, the customary day for commemorating the deceased. Additionally, they supported frequent reception of holy communion and practiced unceasing prayer of the heart.

Theological renewal, liturgical ressourcement, frequent communion, and the Jesus prayer were the emblems of this revival. The Orthodox response to Enlightenment works like Diderot's *Encyclopedia* was an anthology of writings on prayer. The *Philokalia*, published in Venice

---

9 This term refers to the transformation of the substance of the bread and wine into the substance of the body and blood of Christ, while preserving their original external characteristics.

in 1782 by Makarios Notaras, Metropolitan of Corinth (1731-1805), and Saint Nicodemus the Hagiorite (1749-1809) had a profound influence on the Orthodox faithful, particularly with its promotion of the Jesus prayer. The *Philokalia* would also have a major impact on the Russian spiritual renaissance of the nineteenth century.

> **Orthodoxy and ecumenism**
>
> *The term "ecumenism" refers to the quest for Christian unity. The Orthodox Church was one of the pioneers of ecumenism. While it considers itself the "one holy, catholic, and apostolic Church," it is also committed to Christ's commandements "That they may all be one" (John 17:21). In the early twentieth century, the Ecumenical Patriarchate published an encyclical calling for the creation of an institution to bring together the different Christian churches and communities on the model of the League of Nations. This organization, the World Council of Churches, was finally formed in 1948.*
>
> *The ecumenical movement is also made up of different bilateral initiatives. In other words, Orthodoxy has official theological commissions with numerous other Churches. The most significant of these is certainly its bilateral commission with the Catholic Church. This commission, which was made possible by the rapprochement between Ecumenical Patriarch Athenagoras and Pope Paul VI during their meeting in Jerusalem in 1964, has met regularly since the early 1980s.*[10]
>
> *While some traditionalist currents within Orthodoxy oppose ecumenical endeavors, the majority of Orthodox Churches are committed to dialog and to efforts to restore Christian unity by re-establishing communion with other Churches.*

---

10 Chryssavgis, John (ed.), *Dialogue of Love: Breaking the Silence of Centuries* (New York, NY: Fordham University Press, 2014).

The rise of Slavic Orthodoxy

The heir of Byzantium

After the fall of the Byzantine Empire, Russia took up its mantle as its heir. The connection between Byzantium and Russia dated back to the ninth century, when Byzantine missionaries led by the brothers Saints Cyril and Methodius had set out to convert the Slavs, and it was in Byzantium that the princes of Kyiv found a faith for their people. The baptism of Prince Vladimir, which led to the "baptism of the Rus" in 988, imposed Christianity as the official religion of his principality. Kyiv, which had become one of the great European cities, began to imitate the Byzantine Empire. Vladimir's son Yaroslav the Wise (1036-1054) built the cathedral of Saint Sophia in Kyiv. The expansion of the principality of Kyiv, and with it the Orthodox Church, was challenged by successive invasions, the most serious of which was the Mongol invasion. Kyiv was sacked repeatedly, forcing its princes to move their capital to Vladimir and then, in the fourteenth century, to Moscow. The seat of the Church was also moved to Moscow, where it became independent from Constantinople. In Moscow, the Russian princes began to call themselves "tsars," a Russian form of Caesar. With this change in title, proof of the acculturation of Christianity and Orthodoxy in Russia, Moscow was hailed as the Third Rome. In keeping with this growth in stature, the Church of Moscow became a Patriarchate at the end of the sixteenth century.

Church and State: the synodal era

In the sixteenth century, the religious future of Russia was disputed by two different movements. One was represented by Joseph of Volokolmansk (1440-1515), who favored a close relationship between the political authorities and the Church, giving the latter the right to administer immense estates whose revenues would be dedicated to charity and education. His chief opponent was Nilus of Sora (1433-1508), who preached the virtues of poverty and independence from the State. Saint Nilus was ultimately proven right by the growing secularization of the Russian Empire from the eighteenth century onwards. The drive towards secularization was particularly marked under Peter the Great (1682-1725), whose reforms transformed Orthodoxy in Russia. The most visible of these reforms was a change in ecclesiastical administration. While the Russian Orthodox Church had previously been headed by a patriarch, Peter the Great replaced him with a synod, a collegial body under State authority inspired by the leadership model of Protestant Churches.

> **Peter the Great's reforms**
>
> *Peter the Great aimed to modernize Russia with a sweeping set of reforms that were strongly influenced by the West. These changes were forced on Russian society. The army was reorganized, the court system was overhauled, and on the religious front, after the death of the Patriarch Adrian in 1700, the tsar refused to appoint a successor and instead formed the Holy Synod to run the Church's affairs.*

It is essential to grasp the scale of this reform. It profoundly altered the nature of the Church's administration and inaugurated what is known as the "synodal period" marked by the abolition of the Patriarchate, which would end only with the beginning of the Russian Revolution in 1917. As the tsarist regime was transformed and then replaced by the Communists, control of the Church by the State fell into new hands, leaving the Church at the mercy of a new tormentor. While it was often seen as just another cog in the state machine, the Russian Orthodox Church of the nineteenth century put tremendous energy into studying the reforms that would be required to face the modern world. This dynamism was enabled by the fact that Tsar Nicholas II (1894-1918) had granted freedom of movement and speech in a constitution, leading to the Council of Moscow in 1917-1918, which reaffirmed the independence of the Orthodox Church. The council's emblematic achievement was the restoration of the patriarchate and the elevation of Metropolitan Tikhon of Moscow as patriarch.

This period of calm was short-lived, however, since the Russian Revolution was already raging. The Revolution soon came to oppose religion, following in the footsteps of Marx, who called it "the opium of the people." Marxism had defined Western Christianity as an aspect of class struggle. In Russia, however, the context was very different. Unlike in the West, the lower classes were far more devout than the highly secularized upper classes.

To fully comprehend the resurgence of religion in Russia and the rebirth of the Orthodox Church in the late twentieth century as one of the most dynamic in the Orthodox world, we must first understand the terrible measures faced by the Church under Communism. Separation of Church and State was officially recognized by the decree of January 1918. This was followed by restrictive measures against the Church, particularly in terms of property rights, as the Church was denied any legal status, even as an association. Accusations of disturbing the peace were often used to put the Church on the wrong side of the law. Religious buildings were destroyed and monastics and priests were sent to the gulag. This policy of persecution continued, at least on paper, until the fall of the Berlin Wall in 1989 and the dismemberment of the USSR in the early 1990s. The religious revival that followed the fall of communism was a true resurrection for Orthodox Christianity.

| Faith and culture

The 1782 publication of the *Philokalia*, an anthology of the Church Fathers' writings on prayer, completed the victory of hesychasm. It also marked the beginning of a vast cultural renaissance. In Russia, this revival was expressed in the nineteenth century rediscovery of Orthodoxy by intellectuals like Dostoevsky and sparked a sweeping ressourcement. While the Bolshevik Revolution decapitated the movement in Russia, the revival continued in exile in Paris and New York before returning to traditionally Orthodox countries after 1989.

Although its structure was subject to the State, the Russian Orthodox Church, and more specifically Russian piety, had a strong influence on the literary and philosophical culture of the empire that was particularly inspired by the traditional Orthodox respect for monasticism. Russian literature features many religious characters who can only be understood through faith, and thus serves as a source of inspiration that marks daily life with emblems of Orthodoxy. The greatest literary example is Dostoevsky, who in his novel *The Brothers Karamazov* modeled the Elder Zosima on a real elder recognized as a saint by the Orthodox Church, Ambrose of Optina (1812-1881).

The same period also produced the greatest of all Russian saints, Seraphim of Sarov (1759-1833). After entering a monastery as a teenager, Saint Seraphim retired to the depths of the woods to live a life of extremely strict asceticism. He had a profound influence on his visitors. During one such memorable visit, he reminded one of his spiritual children, Nicholas Motovilov, of the necessity of acquiring the Holy Spirit and the deification of the human person.

> *However important prayer, fasting, vigil and all the other Christian practices may be, they do not constitute the aim of our Christian life. Although it is true that they serve as the indispensable means of reaching this end, the true aim of our Christian life consists of the acquisition of the Holy Spirit of God. As for fasts, and vigils, and prayer, and almsgiving, and every good deed done for Christ's sake, they are the only means of acquiring the Holy Spirit of God.*
>
> St. Seraphim of Sarov

| The Orthodox diaspora

| Dispersion of the Orthodox faithful

Today, Orthodoxy is putting down roots worldwide in the new context of the "diaspora." While it is geographically and culturally eastern, Orthodoxy now has a strong presence in many other countries. Mass immigration in the twentieth and twenty-first centuries spread Orthodox Christians throughout the West, from Western Europe to North America and Australia. Virtually all the autocephalous Orthodox Churches are now represented in the diaspora – in other words, outside their canonical territory. Orthodox communities in countries where their presence is relatively recent are generally organized along ethno-national and jurisdictional lines.

> **The Orthodox diaspora**
>
> *The diaspora is a key concern for contemporary Orthodoxy. The issue at stake is both broader and deeper than the dispersion of Orthodox populations outside their traditional territories and the jurisdictions of the autocephalous Orthodox Churches. It is also a systemic ecclesiological issue because the existence of multiple Orthodox dioceses on the same territory is a direct violation of the principles that organize Orthodox communities, which are based on the rule of one bishop, one territory, and one Eucharist. In response to these concerns, the Holy and Great Council of the Orthodox Church (Crete, 2016) addressed the question of the diaspora, offering a temporary solution in the form of regional assemblies of bishops. The Holy and Great Council confirmed the creation of thirteen regions for that purpose.*
>
> *These assemblies of bishops are resources for local coordination and cooperation and facilitate pan-Orthodox cooperation.*

Orthodoxy in America

Origins

It is believed that the first Orthodox Christians in America were Greek immigrants who established a colony near St. Augustine, Florida in 1768. A building where these immigrants held religious services still stands today and is now St. Photios Shrine under the care of the Greek Orthodox Archdiocese of America. Another significant early presence of Orthodoxy in America began with eight missionaries from the Valaamo Monastery in Russia who arrived in Kodiak, Alaska in 1794. These Russian missionaries built Orthodox churches and led many indigenous Alaskans to embrace Orthodoxy.

Following these early settlements of Orthodox Christians, Orthodoxy in America grew rapidly as large waves of Orthodox Christians emigrated to the U.S to begin new lives. In the 1860s, the first Orthodox parishes outside of Alaska emerged to support faithful immigrant communities. From the 1890s through World War I, immigration of Orthodox Christians from Eastern Europe and the Mediterranean soared while simultaneously Eastern Rite Catholics in America converted to Orthodoxy in great numbers through the Russian Church. These immigrants formed ethnic enclaves to gather funds, hire a priest from their home country, and found parishes.

As the numbers of Orthodox parishes increased, there was a growing need for institutional oversight and support. Greek Orthodox parishes in America were unified through the establishment of the Greek Orthodox Archdiocese of North and South America by the Ecumenical Patriarchate in 1922. Russian Orthodox parishes in America were first organized under the Moscow Patriarchate. Through decades of political change in Europe including the Bolshevik Revolution in 1917 and two World Wars, the organization of Orthodox churches in America evolved into the ethnic jurisdictions of Orthodox communities which still exist today.

The Orthodox mosaic

Presently, the jurisdictions of Orthodox Christianity in the United States span eight of the globally recognized autocephalous, or administratively self-governing, Churches which together comprise Eastern Orthodoxy. From these eight jurisdictions come twelve regional dioceses:

- Under the Ecumenical Patriarchate of Constantinople are four U.S. churches: the Greek Orthodox Archdiocese of America, the American Carpatho-Russian Orthodox Diocese of the USA, the Ukrainian Orthodox Church of the USA, and the Albanian Orthodox Diocese.

- Under the Patriarchate of Antioch, there is the Antiochian Orthodox Christian Archdiocese of North America.

- Under the Patriarchate of Moscow there are two recognized churches: the Moscow Patriarchal Parishes in the USA and the Russian Orthodox Church Outside of Russia (ROCOR).

- Under the Patriarchate of Serbia, there is the Serbian Orthodox Church in North, Central, and South America.

- Under the Patriarchate of Romania, there is the Romanian Orthodox Metropolia of the Americas.

- Under the Patriarchate of Bulgaria, there is the Bulgarian Eastern Orthodox Diocese of the USA, Canada, and Australia.

- Under the Patriarchate of Georgia, there is the Georgian Apostolic Orthodox Church in North America.

- And finally, there is the self-governing Orthodox Church in America, which was formerly the Russian Orthodox Greek Catholic Church of North America under the Patriarchate of Moscow. The Orthodox Church in America was granted autocephaly by the Moscow Patriarchate in 1970. Its autocephaly is not recognized by all the Autocephalous Orthodox Churches, but is in communion with most of them.

In numbers, this Eastern Orthodox mosaic in the United States includes over 2,000 parishes across all jurisdictions. There are approximately 1 million Orthodox Christians in the United States today. Given the ethnic origins and immigrant composition of all Orthodox churches in the United States, the population of Orthodox Christians is more heavily concentrated in certain areas where migrant communities settled and thrived. For example, almost half of all Orthodox Christians live in just five states: California, New York, New Jersey, Florida, and Illinois.

While it is important to recognize the immigrant origins of Orthodoxy in the United States and the resulting ethnic jurisdictions, it must be emphasized that Orthodoxy today is not limited to ethnic enclaves. Over decades, thousands of American converts have joined Orthodox churches, many of whom worship in English as well as the immigrant community's native language. Most converts come from Protestant Christianity and are enveloped into the Orthodox Christian family. Generations later, there are now American Orthodox Christians born into the Church who have no ethnic connection to Orthodoxy as their parents and grandparents converted before them.

Orthodox Unity: From SCOBA to the Assembly of Bishops

While ethnic jurisdictions in American Orthodoxy are a reality today, their collaboration manifests the bond of communion that unites them. There has long been discussion amongst Orthodox Christians in the U.S. about better coordinating their work and witnessing to the unity of Orthodoxy as well as about better answering the pastoral needs of the faithful. The first concentrated effort to achieve this goal was initiated in 1965 by the creation of the Standing Conference of the Canonical Orthodox Bishops in the Americas (SCOBA). This body brought together Orthodox hierarchs in the U.S. and Canada for the purpose of discussing shared challenges and goals in shaping the future of Orthodoxy in America.

SCOBA was succeeded in 2010 by the Assembly of Canonical Orthodox Bishops of the United States of America which includes all active, canonical Orthodox bishops in the U.S. of every jurisdiction. Having assumed SCOBA's agencies, ministries, and dialogue, the Assembly is tasked with working toward and fostering unity. Established in accordance with the decision of the Fourth Pre-Conciliar Pan-Orthodox Conference in Chambésy, Switzerland in 2009, the Assembly is both consultative and programmatic. It is both a platform for dialogue which enables the exchange of ideas and best practices among faith leaders in America across jurisdictions and a means to execute pastoral care and programs which minister to the American faithful in a unified manner. The Assembly is, in its mission, a transitional body: "The Assembly ultimately aims to dissolve when it can successfully be succeeded by a governing Synod of a united Orthodox Church in the United States."[11]

---

11 www.assemblyofbishops.org

| Key points

- During the second millennium, the center of gravity of Orthodoxy shifted. The domination of the Mediterranean basin by the Muslim Ottoman Empire led to ecclesiastical and theological changes that have profoundly marked Orthodox life ever since. The influence of the Catholic and Protestant Christian West became increasingly strong as Orthodoxy adapted to its minority position in a changing world.

- With the disappearance of the Byzantine Empire, Orthodoxy grew stronger in Slavic countries, particularly imperial Russia. The Communist era was one of the most severe periods of persecution of Christianity. After the fall of the Berlin Wall in 1989, the Russian Orthodox Church experienced an extraordinary renewal. The number of churches in Russia continues to increase. However, the temptation to instrumentalize religion for political ends remains very present.

- New waves of migration continue to spread Orthodoxy outside its traditional, canonical territories. The diaspora is a major challenge in terms of both pan-Orthodox collaboration and the theological definitions that form the basis of the principles of unity and communion within Orthodoxy.

PART 2
The Heart of Orthodoxy

|Chapter 4
Orthodox Doctrine

IN THIS CHAPTER

- The Trinity
- Humanity
- The Church

To understand what the Orthodox Church is, we must first understand what it believes. Some authors, like Metropolitan Kallistos (Ware) of Diokleia, define Orthodoxy as the "Church of the seven Ecumenical Councils."

In other words, the principles that constitute the Orthodox faith are rooted in the development of Christian dogma, which mainly took place during the first millennium. Dogmas are not considered inventions but a process of growth from a single source: Tradition, in the sense of transmission, which is expressed through the Scriptures, the canons, the councils, and the teaching of the Church Fathers.

The Trinity

The existence of the Trinity is an essential revelation of the Christian faith – one which does not, however, exhaust the transcendence of God who is one in three persons, the living God, the savior God. The theology of the Trinity was developed mainly in the fourth century in the works of the Cappadocian Fathers (Saints Basil the Great, Gregory of Nyssa, and Gregory of Nazianzus, also known as the Theologian). Saint Gregory the Theologian wrote in very striking terms:

> *Above all guard for me this great deposit of faith for which I live and fight, which I want to take with me as a companion, and which makes me bear all evils and despise all pleasures: I mean the profession of faith in the Father and the Son and the Holy Spirit. I entrust it to you today. By it I am soon going to plunge you into water and raise you up from it. I give it to you as the companion and patron of your whole life. I give you but one divinity and power, existing one in three, and containing the three in a distinct way. Divinity without disparity of substance or nature, without superior degree that raises up or inferior degree that casts down... the infinite co-naturality of three infinites. Each person considered in himself is entirely God... the three considered together... I have not even begun to think of unity when the Trinity bathes me in its splendor. I have not even begun to think of the Trinity when unity grasps me.*

| One God...

The Orthodox Church believes that there is no contradiction between the oneness of God and the Trinity because it affirms that God is one essence in three persons or hypostases. Even this distinction, however, cannot entirely pierce the mystery of God. It is impossible to know what God is except as the One revealed to the world in the Scriptures.

To avoid enclosing the concept of God in a mesh of restrictive intellectual formulas, Orthodox theologians prefer negative, or "apophatic," theology – defining God by what He is balanced by the recognition of the theological limits of language itself. God is great. God is all-powerful. But God is also above all grandeur and above all power. Seeking to approach the nature of God means enclosing it in the limits of our own knowledge. Apophatic theology respects the absolute transcendence of God while reminding us that, as Evagrius Ponticus and Saint Dionysios the Areopagite wrote in the fourth and sixth centuries, respectively, contemplation goes beyond reason and leads to deification.

The oneness of God is where "negative" and "positive" approaches to theology meet. God is both fully beyond and fully within Creation. He allows us to participate in and discover Him not only through intellectual exercises, but also through the experience of the grace communicated through the sacraments and life of the Church – and yet, He is both inapproachable and incomprehensible.

...in Three Persons

God is one in essence. This single nature of God – unknowable, imparticipable, indivisible – does not exist outside the three persons of the Trinity, the Father, the Son, and the Holy Spirit. These three persons do not exist individually, in other words separately from the others, but in a movement of absolute love. Because, as Metropolitan Kallistos writes, "God is not only a unity but a union."[12] And yet the indissoluble tie that unites them does not diminish their individual characteristics.

The Father

The Father is a mysterious figure, and certainly the person of the Trinity who best wears the mantle of transcendence. The "Eternal One" of the Old Testament appears in the background of the New Testament. Jesus constantly evokes his Fatherhood, in both the events of his life and his teaching. In the Gospel according to John, Jesus bears witness to him, saying,

> *As the Father has loved me, so I have loved you; abide in my love. If you keep my commandments, you will abide in my love, just as I have kept my Father's commandments and abide in his love.*
>
> John 15:9-10

---

12 Ware, Kallistos, The Orthodox Church, op.cit.

The Creed of Nicaea-Constantinople also speaks of Him in succinct terms: "The Father almighty, creator of Heaven and Earth," from whom the Son, who is "consubstantial" with Him (of the same nature) was "begotten before all ages," and from whom the Holy Spirit proceeds. He is both origin and principle. Very little is affirmed about Him, out of respect for His omnipotence. The Father is traditionally never represented in Orthodox iconography. He only began to be represented relatively recently, under the influence of Western art.

| The Son, God incarnate

God as Trinity is a central revelation that came with the incarnation of Jesus Christ. Jesus Christ is recognized as the Logos, the second person of the Trinity, the Son, who, by taking flesh from the Virgin Mary, revealed the existence of the Father and the Holy Spirit. It was to answer the question "Who is Jesus?" that all of the Ecumenical Councils were convened. In 325, the Council of Nicaea declared that Jesus is God because he shares the divine nature of the Father. The Creed of Nicaea-Constantinople (325-381) declared that He is "consubstantial" with the Father. The Councils of Ephesus (431) and Chalcedon (451) sought to understand the relationship between the human nature and the divine nature in the hypostasis, or person, of Christ, who is both fully man and fully God. In the words of the Chalcedonian Creed:

> We, then, following the holy Fathers, all with one consent, teach men to confess one and the same Son, our Lord Jesus Christ, the same perfect in Godhead and also perfect in manhood; truly God and truly man [...] consubstantial with the Father according to the Godhead, and consubstantial with us according to Humanity [...] one and the same Christ, Son, Lord, only begotten, to be acknowledged in two natures, inconfusedly, unchangeably, indivisibly, inseparably..."

The incarnation is the ultimate expression of God's love for humanity and for all of Creation. The incarnation is also the means of salvation. Following Adam's sin and fall, death and sin separated human beings from God. Only God could reopen the doors of communion. Through the incarnation, God entered time and history. He took on flesh and bore Creation, taking on our human condition. He shared in our humanity, which He received from His mother. Jesus was born with no human father by the action of the grace of the Holy Spirit. He was conceived on the day of the Annunciation, when the Archangel Gabriel told Mary that she would have a son without having sexual relations (Luke 1:24-38). In that moment, the entire universe was turned on its head: the source of life came into the heart of Creation. In the words of Saint Irenaeus of Lyon, Jesus "recapitulates" in himself all of humanity. Jesus is the new Adam through whom salvation enters the world. By his voluntary self-emptying (*kenosis*) of His transcendence as God in favor of immanence, Christ allows us to encounter Him, and through that encounter unites the human and the divine.

> **The Virgin Mary**
>
> *In the Orthodox tradition, since the Third Ecumenical Council (Ephesus, 431), the Virgin Mary has been called the Theotokos, or Mother of God. This title highlights not only her role in the history of salvation but also the divine reality of her Son. She gave birth to the second person of the Holy Trinity, who through her took on a nature identical to our own. The term Theotokos is not only an honorific. It is also a confession of faith in God made man, Jesus Christ, who is consubstantial with the Father. Mary is also called "All Holy" because she is the most perfect of human beings. God gave her the freedom to decide whether or not to be the instrument of salvation. She remained a virgin through the conception and birth of Christ and throughout her life. In iconography, this is symbolized by the three stars that appear on her mantle: one on her forehead and two on her shoulders.*[13]

According to Orthodox theology, this union of the human and the divine is made possible in the person of Christ. It is referred to as the "hypostatic," or more simply "personal," union. The Council of Chalcedon (451) dug deeper into the meaning of the union of Christ's fully human and fully divine natures, adding a crucial precision: "inconfusedly, unchangeably, indivisibly, inseparably." Through His

---

[13] More generally on the subject of the Theotokos: Schmemann, Alexander, *The Virgin Mary – Celebration of Faith*, vol.III (St. Vladimir's Seminary Press, 1995).

incarnation, the Logos, Jesus Christ, took on our nature which was tainted by the fall to transfigure it and perfect it through the ultimate sacrifice of the cross and the life-giving power of His Resurrection.

The Holy Spirit

The third person of the Trinity is indissociable from the two others. The mission of the Holy Spirit, like that of the Son, is to fulfill the will of the Father, continuing Jesus's work in the gathering of the faithful, the Church. Within the Trinity, the Holy Spirit is equal to the other two persons, the Father and the Son, but proceeds only from the Father. Christians believe that the Holy Spirit is mentioned in the biblical account of creation, sweeping over the water (Gen. 1:2). The Patristic tradition sees the Holy Spirit's unique role as "perfecting" through sanctification, or "consoling" in the sense of the Gospel according to John:

> *When the Consoler comes, whom I will send to you from the Father, the Spirit of truth who comes from the Father, he will testify on my behalf. You also are to testify, because you have been with me from the beginning.*

John 15:26-27

As the Spirit of communion that transforms the world and unites humanity to God, the Holy Spirit represents the fulfillment of the Christian vocation.

Humanity

Humanity is one of God's creations, according to the beginning of the book of Genesis. It plays a central role in creation, not only as a steward but also as a servant. This understanding of the human place in creation also explains the direction taken by Orthodox ecology over the past three decades.

Image and likeness

Human beings, men and women alike, are created "in the image and likeness of God" (Gen. 1:26). These two biblical principles are both static and dynamic. The image of God is a gift to all of humanity, which Orthodox theology understands as human freedom and dignity. Likeness, on the other hand, corresponds to our spiritual vocation of union with God. It can be understood as free will in action, inspired by grace.

Despite these gifts, humanity in the persons of Adam and Eve turned away from God. Their choice led to the fall, to death, and to suffering.

| The Fall

It was of his own free will that the first man turned away from God to follow the path of evil, rather than good. In doing so, he not only set himself in opposition to God but also caused the emergence of consequences that violated his original nature: corruption, death, disease, and more. Humanity has inherited the consequences of Adam's sin (Romans 5:12 et seq.).

Here, it is important to highlight the difference between the Orthodox and Western Christian interpretations of what is often referred to as "original sin." As Fr. John Meyendorff has demonstrated, based on the teachings of the Church Fathers, each human person is responsible for his or her own sins and cannot be guilty of sins committed by someone else, even Adam. However, all of humanity does bear the consequences of original sin: it is subject to death and constantly exposed to sin and temptation. Sin has not blotted out the image of God, only tarnished and deformed it. Human freedom is one of the characteristics of the image of God and remains open to encounters, synergy, and collaboration with God, turning us back towards goodness, the source of divine life. Sin has, however, corrupted the human ability to desire union with God. Since we are no longer able to turn to God, or even capable of wanting to do so, it is God who takes the first step.

| Synergy

By *synergy*, the Apostle Paul means cooperation with God: "For we are God's coworkers, working together" (1 Cor. 3:9). God cannot be reached by our desire alone. He has to allow it, make himself available, and enable us to turn to Him. According to Metropolitan Kallistos, the Virgin Mary typifies this convergence between God's will to save and the human will to be saved. That encounter occured in Mary's "yes" on the day of the Annunciation, when the Archangel Gabriel brought her the news that she would have a son, the Son of God. In the fourth century, Saint Macarius of Egypt wrote:

> *But you are created in the image and likeness of God because, as God is free and creates what he wills, so, too, are you free.*

The idea of human cooperation with divine grace is not accepted by all Christian confessions. However, it is based on the teachings of the Church Fathers, who, in the early years of the first millennium, fully understood the asymmetry and the independence of God relative to human free will.

| Deification

| Humanity and divinity

Christ accomplishes in himself the union of all of humanity with God, re-establishing the original relationship offered to human beings on the day of Creation and giving this union a totalizing dimension, from redemption and salvation to deification (*theosis*), the human vocation to become God through grace. In the words of Fr. John Meyendorff,

> *In "deification," man achieves the supreme goal for which he is created. This goal, already realized in Christ by a unilateral action of God's love, represents both the meaning of human history and a judgment over man. It is open to man's response and free effort.*[14]

The Church Fathers, including Saint Irenaeus of Lyon in the late second century and Saint Athanasius the Great in the fourth century, are known for the expression: "God became man so that man might become God." Through salvation, humanity is incorporated into the divine. It bears not only the image of the one God, but the image of God the Trinity because the deification of human beings is, in fact, union with God. This union is called "mystical," unlike the union of

---

14 Meyendorff, John, *Byzantine Theology: Historical Trends and Doctrinal Themes* (Fordham University, 1983).

the three persons of the Trinity, because the distinction between the Creator and the created remains clear. No matter how strong our relationship with God, our humanity never disappears. The human person remains distinct from God by its nature while participating in God's grace. In other words, as he or she becomes God by grace, the human person still remains human in nature. Deification is offered to everyone.

The body

According to Orthodox teaching, grace transfigures not only the soul but also the body. The human person is understood as a whole, so the body participates in the deification of the entire person. This explains the major significance of the relics of saints in Orthodox piety and worship. The Orthodox approach to relics is not about magic or even miracles: relics, both incorrupt bodies and bones, are venerated because the Orthodox Church recognizes the holiness of the person whose body is already experiencing the glory that risen bodies will experience on the last day by anticipation, because of his or her closeness with God. While the saints are holy, they are not perfect. In fact, they are keenly aware of their own limitations. This respect for the body, in which the image and likeness of God are inscribed and with its potential for holiness, also explains why the Orthodox Church opposes cremation.

The environment

Renewed humanity is united with Christ's economy, bringing all of creation with it. It is carried towards God by the act of making an offering, thanking God for the invisible transformation of the world, whose profound orientation has been changed from death to life. The world that was lost has now been transfigured.

The stewardship of creation entrusted to humanity (Gen. 2:15) is the theological basis on which Orthodoxy has developed a prophetic environmental message over the past three decades. In 1989, Ecumenical Patriarch Dimitrios (1972-1991) published the first encyclical on the protection of the environment, establishing September 1 as the "Day of Prayer for the Protection of the Environment." Today, following in his footsteps, Ecumenical Patriarch Bartholomew emphasizes an ascetic approach to nature based on the recognition that the destruction of nature is not only a moral crisis but also a direct result of sin. The Orthodox environmental approach, which sees in the environment and nature the hand of God laid open to contemplation *(physiki théoria)*, also addresses the social aspect of *theosis*.

We are not saved alone. The source of salvation is a close relationship with God, which shapes our relationships with our neighbors and with our broader environment.

| The Church

The Orthodox Church identifies itself as the "one, holy, catholic and apostolic Church" of the creed of Nicaea-Constantinople. It is simultaneously the reality of communion with God and the manifestation of His Kingdom, the body of Christ, a social body, and an event which continues the work of Christ and the experience of Pentecost. The Church was founded by the descent of the Holy Spirit on the apostles. Etymologically, the Church is a community of those who have been called, uniting different people.

| An icon of the Trinity

The Trinity shapes Orthodox ecclesiology as well as Christian anthropology. The parallel between Church and Trinity lies in the articulation of unity and diversity. The unity of communion *(koinonia)* that constitutes the Church does not abolish the individual diversity of the baptized believers who form the body of the Church. The oneness of the Church is in each person, as a member of the body of Christ, and each person is in its oneness. The interdependence of the one and the many is covered by the concept of the catholicity of the Church. In Orthodox teaching, the term "catholicity" refers not only to Orthodoxy as a confession or to universality in a geographical sense, but to the simultaneousness of the one and the whole, based on the principle of the Trinity. The Church is thus made up of baptized individuals not on the basis of a hierarchy, despite the hierarchical structure of the Church, but on the basis of charisms, drawing on the different talents, gifts, and functions offered by the members of the Church for its service and growth. These gifts include holy orders: service as a bishop, priest, or deacon. The importance of the diversity of the Church is underscored by the fact that a priest cannot celebrate the Divine Liturgy alone. He must be accompanied by at least one other person who represents the community's diversity in unity, echoing Christ's words: "For where two or three are gathered in my name, I am there among them." (Matthew 18:20).

The body of Christ

The use of the expression "the body of Christ" to refer to the Church dates back to the Apostle Paul: "so we, who are many, are one body in Christ, and individually we are members of one another." (Romans 12:5) The image of the body is not only a way to express the concept of unity and diversity. It also expresses the continuation of Christ's incarnation in History as a community in which the union of the human and the divine continues to be effected. It is within the Church that humanity participates most fully in God's holiness.

Participating in the sacraments of the Church is what enables human beings to experience the Body of Christ in the Church. Through baptism, Christians participate in Christ's death and resurrection. Through chrismation, they receive the gift of the Holy Spirit, which consecrates them to receive the body and blood of Christ in the Eucharist. The Eucharist, as it unites us to Christ, also unites us to each other. This is why the Eucharist is so central for Orthodoxy. It is a principle of unity, the grace through which the entire world is sanctified.

The Church of the Holy Spirit

The Church is also the space in which the Holy Spirit perfects the work of the Son. The Holy Spirit inhabits the body of Christ and sanctifies the faithful. The Church of the Spirit grows in the Spirit of the Church. It is the Spirit of truth and freedom that was revealed at Pentecost when the tongues of fire descended on the disciples, according to the Acts of the Apostles. The Spirit is offered to the Church as a gift, granted to every person who is baptized and uniting the visible and the invisible. The Church, the body of Christ, is both divine and human as He is.

The Holy Spirit unites the universal – catholic, in the etymological sense of the term – Church to the local Church through participation in the Eucharistic sacrifice. The Eucharistic consecration prayer calls on the Holy Spirit to descend both on the gifts, making them the body and blood of Christ, and on the entire liturgical community. The action of the Holy Spirit in the divine liturgy transcends the separation between the visible and the invisible, making them a single, united reality within the body of Christ, the Church. While the Church is made up of saints and angelic powers, the imperfect human reality of the local embodiment of the Church generates a contradictory tension that invites the imperfect and sinful members of the Church to be transformed by grace.

| Unity, primacy and conciliarity

The Church is one because God is one. The Church is one because there is only one body of Christ. In Orthodoxy, unlike Catholicism, the principal that maintains the visible unity of the Church is not the pope. Instead, it is sacramental communion in the body and blood of Christ through the celebration of the divine liturgy. *Koinonia* – communion – exists within each local community, each Eucharistic assembly gathered around its bishop, who delegates priests to celebrate the Eucharist in his absence. The Orthodox Church is thus a communion of local churches in which the bishop is the guarantor of the Eucharist within each local church. The bishop presides over the Eucharist in which the faithful participate by receiving communion. Communion among bishops, and the communion of the faithful in the Eucharist presided by the bishop, are the manifestation of the unity of the Church.[15]

---

15 Cf. Zizioulas, John, *Eucharist, Bishop, Church : The Unity of the Church in the Divine*

The thirty-fourth apostolic canon explains this relationship:

> *The bishops of every nation must acknowledge him who is first among them and account him as their head, and do nothing of consequence without his consent; but each may do those things only which concern his own parish, and the country places which belong to it. But neither let him (who is the first) do anything without the consent of all; for so there will be unanimity, and God will be glorified through the Lord in the Holy Spirit.*

Orthodox theology thus affirms that the Church is one and true because it has preserved its doctrine and the authenticity of its religious experience intact. Echoing Cyprian of Carthage (200-258), it also teaches that "outside the Church, there is no salvation," although the borders of the Church are often porous and God's grace is free to act outside them.

The bishop directs, teaches, and presides over the sacraments of his church, which is made up of the other charisms, both ordained (priesthood and diaconate) and lay (the people of God or *laos*). The interdependence of the bishop and of the people of God, who bear the royal priesthood of baptism, is based on the tie of communion that unites them and forges the conciliar nature of the Church. Councils, and especially ecumenical councils, are ecclesiastical events at which the assembled bishops bear witness to their unity and define the doctrinal, pastoral, and canonical contours of Orthodox teaching. Councils must, however, be received by the faithful to be accepted.

While the Church is conciliar in nature, primacy does exist on three levels: local, regional within each autocephalous Church, and global on the pan-Orthodox scale. Pan-Orthodox primacy was made particularly tangible by the Holy and Great Council of 2016. The Ecumenical Patriarchate of Constantinople is recognized as holding this form of primacy, known as *primus inter pares* (first among equals). In Orthodox theology, there is no conciliarity without primacy and no primacy without conciliarity

---

Eucharist and the Bishop during the First Three Centuries (Holy Cross Orthodox Press, 2007).

> **The End of Time**
>
> *Orthodox Christians live in the expectation of the resurrection of the dead and eternal life. This eschatology – the accomplishment of the last things – does not only refer to the coming of the Kingdom of God for the righteous and hell for the damned. It is also the consummation of all time when Christ returns. Orthodoxy teaches that the second coming of Christ remains imminent, highlighting the continual state of expectation in which Christians live. The last things are already present in the liturgy.*

Key points

- Orthodox theology, in the sense of discourse about God, is shaped by the existence of the Trinity. God is one in three persons, in the communion of love of the Father, Son, and Holy Spirit. Each of the three persons of the Trinity is fully God and yet has personal attributes that distinguish it from the other two persons. The Father is unbegotten, the Son is begotten by the Father, and the Holy Spirit proceeds from the Father alone.

- Humanity is a creation of God, which God seeks to save through Christ's incarnation. "God became man so that man might become God." Human beings are created in the image and likeness of God: they have free will to choose between communion with God and rejection of the divine. Adam's fall brought corruption into the world. Human nature has therefore inherited the consequences of the sin of Adam and Eve. Orthodoxy affirms that human beings must collaborate with God in their salvation and deification, but this collaboration is enabled by grace.

- Human beings are saved in the Church as the body of Christ through the sanctifying action of the Holy Spirit. Communion is central to the ecclesial experience: communion with God through the Eucharist and communion with the entire Church and all its members. This experience is the source of the synodal and conciliar nature of Orthodoxy. The last things are anticipated within the Church.

Chapter 5
The Church Fathers

> **IN THIS CHAPTER**
>
> - Passing on Tradition
> - The Patristic tradition
> - Hesychasm (fourteenth century)

What is a Church Father? Since Orthodoxy is often considered the Church of the Fathers, that question is primordial. The Church Fathers represent a specific moment in the experience of the transmission of the Christian faith. They are a historical embodiment of the life of the Church, translating the Word of God into time. Their work bears witness to the process of the baptism of cultures that continues today.

Passing on Tradition

The Orthodox Church has an extremely strong sense of tradition. In Greek, the same word means both "tradition" and "transmission." It is important to bear in mind, however, that tradition is not traditionalism, in the sense of fixing the past in the present. On the contrary, in Orthodoxy, Tradition is a dynamic process that takes place in the Church through the inspiration of the Holy Spirit. What does that mean in practice?

Tradition is often compared to both a direction and a journey. Orthodoxy's apparent archaism–its liturgical forms, its organization, and its sacramental practices–are in fact the expression of its millennia of continuity. Tradition is best understood as a process of ecclesiastical development that is a form of faith, rather than merely a set of opinions. The Orthodox faith is founded on the New Testament revelation of Christ fulfilling the Old Covenant and, as the savior God, sacrificing his divinity and his own life for the life of the world. The faith expressed in Orthodox Tradition is rooted in the teachings of Christ, the Apostles, and the Early Church, around which the entire experience of Orthodox spirituality is centered.

In more technical terms, the word Tradition also refers to the specific elements that comprise it. While the following list is not exhaustive, it does highlight the most significant elements of what Orthodoxy seeks to pass down and the foundation on which it stands.

| Holy Scripture

The Bible is a major source of Orthodox tradition, in which God's will is revealed to the world. It is an extremely important source of authority. In Orthodoxy, the Bible's authority is linked to its development within the Church. The Bible cannot be understood apart from Tradition because the process of writing down the teachings of Christ and his Apostles, and later the selection of the books that form the New Testament, took place within the context of the Church and the Councils. The Orthodox share the same New Testament books as all Christians. For the Old Testament, the Greek Septuagint version is considered authoritative.

Scriptural interpretation is a part of the interpretative tradition of Orthodoxy and is best represented by the writings of the Church Fathers. The Bible is also very present in the liturgy. The Psalms, in particular, are central to the prayer of the Church, and the Gospel is read with great solemnity during Orthodox services and venerated with the same fervor as icons.

Dogmas

The definitions of the elements that constitute the Christian faith, particularly those laid down by the Ecumenical Councils, are also a powerful traditional source of authority in Orthodoxy. For example, the Creed of Nicaea-Constantinople and the terms used in it cannot be changed. This creed also occupies a central place in Orthodox services. It is recited every time the divine liturgy is celebrated, not only as confession of faith but also as an act of praise and worship.

Canon law

The canons were developed in the same conciliar context as Orthodox dogmas. The different ecumenical and local canons form a set of rules for Church organization and discipline known as canon law. While Orthodoxy is in many ways less codified than other Christian confessions like Catholicism, its canons do lay out rules governing many aspects of daily life. The canons do not have the same level of authority as dogmas. They were written as practical responses to real-world problems as the need arose. The fasting rules defined by canon law as a branch of tradition are very strict and are still followed by Orthodox Christians today. Other canons are harder to apply in modern life, but interpretations, explanations, and commentaries on them continue to be major sources of inspiration for the study of the canonical tradition. In 1800, the Greek author Nicodemus the Hagiorite published a commentary, *The Rudder*, which is an extremely prolific source of canonical teachings. The strict application of the canons (*akriveia*) is counterbalanced by a more pastoral approach (*economia*) which allows certain exceptions to the rule.

The tradition of the Fathers

It is within the same context of passing on the faith that the Church Fathers contributed to the development of the Church's doctrines, both by taking part in the councils and through their own writings. The Orthodox Church does not have a fixed list of Church Fathers and Mothers. They are identified by the extent to which Orthodoxy is based on their holiness and their impact on the history of the Church. The Church Fathers are not limited to a specific time period, although their Golden Age was essentially in the fourth and fifth centuries. The history of Orthodoxy has been marked by a series of great figures, from Saint Basil the Great in the fourth century to Saint Gregory Palamas in the fourteenth century, and many others in between, including Saint John Chrysostom and Saint Maximus the Confessor.

The term "Patristic conscience" (*consensus patrum*) is often used to refer to the Church Fathers' teachings as a whole. Biblical interpretation is the main focus of their writings.

The teachings of the Church Fathers are particularly important to the Orthodox Church. More than just ancient wisdom, they illustrate how the faith has remained alive throughout history as each of the Fathers translated the faith into the terms of his own era.

The importance of the Church Fathers lies not only in what they wrote but in how they responded to the pressing questions of their day. In a way, they are the embodiment of Tradition–guideposts and lodestars through whom it remains alive and incarnate.

| The patristic tradition

The fourth and fifth centuries are considered the golden age of the Church Fathers. While Orthodox theological thought developed within the framework of the ecclesial conscience as a whole, it is also the product of the individual personalities that shaped the history of Orthodoxy. As the faith spread throughout the Mediterranean basin in the Roman Empire, Christian doctrine began to develop. The Church Fathers did not invent new dogmas; they interpreted eternal truths, making them accessible to their contemporaries. They authored countless ascetic, catechetical, spiritual, didactic, and pastoral works and played a decisive role in the councils, particularly the ecumenical councils.

The vast library of patristic literature offers a rich variety of texts, particularly the works of the men known as the "Doctors" of the Orthodox Church: Ss. Athanasius the Great, Basil the Great, Gregory the Theologian, Gregory of Nyssa, John Chrysostom, Cyril of Alexandria, Maximus the Confessor, and John of Damascus.

Saint Athanasius the Great (328-373)

Ordained Bishop of Alexandria in 328, Saint Athanasius had previously served as a deacon at the Ecumenical Council of Nicaea (325). He is known for his dogmatic, ascetic, and moral writings. His *On the Incarnation* is a direct response to the questions raised by Arianism, which denied the divine nature of Jesus. In it, he powerfully presents the doctrine of the Ecumenical Council of Nicaea, developing the theme of the consubstantiality of the three persons of the Trinity. He also wrote a biography of his contemporary Saint Anthony the Great, the father of monasticism. In his writings on salvation, he demonstrates the reciprocity between God's incarnation and man's deification. We owe to him the famous phrase, which he borrowed from Saint Irenaeus of Lyon, the Word "made Himself man that we might be made God."

Saint Basil the Great (ca. 330-379)

Saint Basil the Great was educated in Athens, where he received the best education available in his day. He put his knowledge and his strong character to work to defend Orthodoxy against Arianism. After he was baptized as an adult, he became the Bishop of Caesarea in Cappadocia in 370. His treatise *On the Holy Spirit* is one of his greatest works. *Saint* Basil died just two years before the second Ecumenical Council (Constantinople, 381) which affirmed the equal dignity of the three persons of the Trinity, including the Holy Spirit. Biblical interpretation was one of his specialties. In the *Hexameron*, he analyzes the Genesis account of the creation of the world. Saint Basil's ascetic writings are no less important. He was the author of the Greater and Lesser Monastic Rules, which still organize the life of monastic communities today. He also wrote the Eucharistic Liturgy that bears his name.

Saint Gregory the Theologian (329-390)

Saint Gregory the Theologian, also known as Saint Gregory of Nazianzus, was a Saint friend of Basil the Great. Like Saint Basil, he was baptized as an adult, at the age of thirty. Saint Gregory was made Bishop of Sassima after refusing multiple times, but was ultimately unable to travel there. Instead, he remained in his father's city of Nazianzus. He later became the Archbishop of Constantinople in 380, under the Emperor Theodosius. As Archbishop, he presided over the Ecumenical Council of Constantinople (381) but returned to Nazianzus before it ended, where he lived out his final years in solitude, working on his voluminous literary output. His writings include numerous orations, the best-known of which are: *Five Theological Orations*, on the doctrine of the Trinity, which inspired his sobriquet of "the Theologian". Saint Gregory's writings are a major source for Orthodox hymnography, particularly the Paschal hymns.

Saint Gregory of Nyssa (ca. 335-ca. 394)

Saint Gregory of Nyssa is known as one of the Cappadocian Fathers, alongside his older brother Saint Basil the Great and Saint Gregory the Theologian. Saint Gregory faithfully expanded on his older brother's thought. His writings include works on biblical interpretation, including *The Life of Moses*, as well as dogmatic treatises on the Trinity such as *Against Eunomus*. He became Bishop of Nyssa in 371 but remained a profoundly mystical author.

Saint John Chrysostom (347-407)

Saint John Chrysostom is, without a doubt, the most prolific of the patristic authors. He was also one of the greatest preachers of his time, leading to his epithet "Chrysostom," or "golden mouth." In 397, he became Archbishop of Constantinople but was later exiled several times for his sermons, which were often fiercely critical of the authorities. He ultimately died alone and abandoned in Comanus, in what is now Abkhazia. Chrysostom's works are far too numerous to list here. He wrote extensive biblical commentaries as well as an endless stream of sermons and letters. His dogmatic works include *On the Incomprehensible Nature of God,* while in his treatise *On the Priesthood,* he was the first to examine the theology of ordination. The liturgy that bears his name is celebrated throughout the year, with the exception of certain feasts and the Sundays of Great Lent when it is replaced by the Liturgy of Saint Basil. Tradition also credits him with the moving Paschal homily that is read every year at the end of the Paschal Matins:

> *If there are devout and God loving people here, let them enjoy this beautiful, radiant festival. If there are prudent servants, enter joyously into the Lord's joy. Whoever may be spent from fasting, enjoy now your reward. [...] No one need lament poverty, for the kingdom is seen as universal. No one need grieve over sins; forgiveness has dawned from the tomb. No one need fear death; the Savior's death has freed us from it [...} Death, where is your sting? Hades, where is your victory? Christ is risen and you are overthrown. Christ is risen and demons have fallen. Christ is risen and angels rejoice. Christ is risen and life rules. Christ is risen and not one dead remains in the tomb. For Christ, having risen from the dead, has become the first fruits of those that slept. To Him be the glory and the dominion forever. Amen.*
>
> Excerpt of the Paschal homily attributed to Saint John Chrysostom

| Saint Cyril of Alexandria (ca. 377-444)

Saint Cyril of Alexandria represents the exegetical school of Alexandria. He was a fierce opponent of the teachings of Nestorius, who held that two persons existed in Christ, one human and the other divine. Saint Cyril defended the position later adopted by the Third Ecumenical Council (Ephesus, 431): that in Christ there is only one person, or hypostasis, the Logos of God in which the human and the divine are united. That inspired the famous formula: "One incarnate nature of God the Word."

> **Exegetical schools**
>
> *The exegetical schools of Alexandria and Antioch developed two different approaches to biblical interpretation. Starting with Origen (185-254), the school of Alexandria used the allegorical method, focusing on the unity of Christ's human and divine natures. The school of Antioch, on the other hand, took a more literal approach to Scripture, emphasizing the difference between Christ's two natures. The Alexandrian school triumphed at the Third Ecumenical Council (Ephesus, 431), while the Antiochian approach was approved by the Fourth Ecumenical Council (Chalcedon, 451).*

Saint Maximus the Confessor (580-662)

Saint Maximus the Confessor authored an authoritative body of dogmatic, moral, ascetic, and mystical writings. In his work *Ambigua*, he explains the difficult passages of Saint Dionysius the Areopagite and Saint Gregory the Theologian. He is particularly famous for his dogmatic writings on the two natures and two wills of Christ.

Saint John of Damascus (ca. 676-749)

The work of Saint John of Damascus synthesized the theology of the Ecumenical Councils, covering a vast scope. In *On the Orthodox Faith*, he summarizes Christian doctrine. He also defended the veneration of sacred images, known as icons. He attacked heresies and often opposed State attempts to intervene in Church affairs.

Hesychasm (fourteenth century)

The debates that rocked fourteenth century Byzantium have profoundly shaped Orthodox theology, particularly monastic spirituality, ever since. The great hesychastic controversy opposed Saint Gregory Palamas (1296-1359), a monk from Mount Athos, and Barlaam of Calabria (ca. 1290-1348), a Greek intellectual from Italy. Their disagreement centered on the knowledge of God. According to Palamas, all baptized Christians can directly access God in Christ. Barlaam, on the other hand, argued that God can be known only through indirect means such as the Scriptures. Tensions escalated when Barlaam attacked the form of prayer practiced by hesychasts. The term hesychast comes from the Greek *hesychia*, or silence. Hesychasts practice the Jesus prayer, the repetition of the few short words "Lord Jesus Christ, Son of God, have mercy on me," often prayed silently. The prayer is combined with breathing practices that enable concentration and attentiveness. Barlaam believed that involving the body in prayer was counterproductive and would in fact disrupt concentration.

While Barlaam's views were condemned by a council in 1341, opponents of hesychasm continued to attack Palamas even after his teachings were approved by councils in 1347 and 1351.

The teachings of Palamas can be summed up as follows:

- The experience of God is granted to all baptized Christians through participation in the sacraments of the Church, particularly baptism and the Eucharist. This experience is neither exclusively material nor exclusively intellectual. All of humanity is deified through prayer, participation in the sacraments, and involvement in the life of the Church, which opens it up to participation in the divine life. As Orthodox theologian Fr. John Meyendorff writes, "knowledge of God implies 'participation' in God."[16]

- God remains entirely inaccessible in His essence. Palamas refined the statement that human beings can become God, adding that this is possible only through grace or participation in the "divine energies." This affirmation protects the transcendence of God and enables us to understand the conditions in which God interacts with His creation, an interaction made possible by His energies, which enable participation in the divine life.

- The purpose of human life is to participate in the life of God – in other words, in deification, where transcendence meets immanence. Palamas was largely inspired by the decisions of the Sixth Ecumenical Council (680). The divine energies are that which is, and thus enable participation in the divine life. In other words, this participation makes human beings more human through communion with God.

---

16 Meyendorff, John, *Byzantine Theology: Historical Trends and Doctrinal Themes*, op.cit.

The life of Saint Gregory Palamas

Saint Gregory Palamas is a central figure in hesychastic theology. Considered a saint by the Orthodox Church, he was born in 1292 to a noble family from Asia Minor that had fled to Constantinople after the Turks invaded the region. After the death of Gregory's father, Emperor Andronicus II Palaiologos (1282-1328) took over responsibility for his education. The young Saint Gregory soon abandoned his classical studies to become a monk. On the advice of his spiritual father Theoleptos of Philadelphia (1250-1326), in about 1316 he left for Mount Athos, where he studied with a hermit during his novitiate before entering the Great Lavra monastery and eventually returning to a life of isolation. Incursions by Turkish pirates drove him to seek refuge in Thessaloniki, where he was ordained a priest in 1326. After returning to Mount Athos sometime around 1331, he became the higumen (abbot) of the Monastery of Esphigmenou. It was at this point in his life that he began to write. In addition to his writings in defense of the hesychasts, he produced treatises opposing the filioque because he could not bear the idea of sacrificing the Orthodox faith to achieve union with the Latin West in the hopes of receiving military aid to resist Ottoman pressure in the east. His theological controversies with Barlaam and Akindynos occurred at a time of religious and political crisis, with John VI Kantakouzenos (1295-1383) facing off against Anna of Savoy (1306-1360), the widow of Emperor Andronicus III (1328-1341). Despite these turbulent times, the theology of Palamas was confirmed by a third council held in Hagia Sophia in 1347 following the victory of John VI Kantakouzenos. In the same year, Palamas was elected and ordained as Metropolitan of Thessalonica. However, the presence of opponents in the city meant that he was not actually installed for several years. The controversy continued to drag on, and Palamite theology was once again approved by the Synodal Tomos of 1351. In 1354, while sailing to Constantinople, Palamas was taken prisoner by the Ottomans. During his captivity, he held the first interreligious

> *dialogue with Islam. After several months, he was freed and returned to Thessalonica, where he died on November 14, 1359. He was canonized very quickly, barely nine years after his death. The second Sunday of Great Lent is dedicated to him in the Orthodox Church.*

| Key points

- While the Church Fathers are the distinctive feature of Orthodoxy, they are never taken in isolation from Tradition as a whole, the Scriptures, the Councils, and canon law–in other words, the life of the Church. Their importance is the direct result of the concept of tradition as the transmission of an ecclesial experience incarnated in time and in history. Through their lives and teachings, the Church Fathers demonstrated the meaning of the Church, baptizing their cultures to enable them to respond to the challenges of their times.

- By striving to live out the spirit of the Fathers and understand the intent and context of their writings, the Orthodox Church has found the keys to spread the Gospel. However, the extremely central position of the Church Fathers can lead to the risk of diminishing the importance of other sources of tradition, particularly the Bible, or locking the Church into a theology of repetition that can become a form of fundamentalism.

- The Fathers and Mothers of the Church are not limited to a specific period. They continue to be a central part of the vitality of Orthodoxy today.

Chapter 6
A Communion of Churches

> **IN THIS CHAPTER**
>
> - The Church as an institution and organization
> - The geopolitics of Orthodoxy
> - The Holy and Great Council (2016)

The Orthodox Church is a communion of fifteen autocephalous (independent) Churches. These Churches are organized locally on the principle of one church, one bishop, one Eucharist. While this principle is not always strictly applied in practice, it is an inheritance from the Early Church that remains in force today. On a practical level, its implementation has been challenged by the expansion of ecclesiastical jurisdictions beyond their traditional, canonical borders due to mass migration in the twentieth century.

At the same time, the Orthodox Church is one united Church. The bond of communion that unites the local Churches and recognition of the apostolic succession of the bishops who lead them connect each local Church to the universal Church. The fact that the Churches share the same Eucharist, the body and blood of Christ, is the foundation and manifestation of their unity as members of the same body. Despite this profound unity, the fusion of religion and national identity in majority-Orthodox regions encourages international alliances and power politics between the local Churches. The Holy and Great Council of June 2016 was intended to increase unity within Orthodoxy by promoting conciliarity, and yet the absence of four Churches from the council highlights the fragility of that unity.

| Institution and organization

| The episcopacy

The Orthodox Church is above all an episcopal church: a church of bishops. In the Early Church, as the Apostles gradually died out, bishops became the guarantors of the gospel message and of the eyewitness accounts of Christ's disciples which are the foundation of the faith. By establishing a principle of continuity, bishops took on an essential role in the transmission of the Christian message, thus developing apostolic succession. Bishops are not only a manifestation of the faith. They also continue and guarantee the faith of the Apostles– here and now– in the life of the Church. While the *episcopos* (bishop) is at the top of the church hierarchy, he cannot be understood outside his role as a preacher and teacher nor his liturgical vocation within the community of which he is an organic part.

Bishops are central to the organization of the Byzantine church first and foremost because they preside over the Divine Liturgy. This liturgical role puts them at the heart of the Church as the bridge between the faith that is professed and the Eucharist that is celebrated. Even today, when a priest celebrates the divine liturgy, he always does so on behalf of the local bishop.

Local jurisdiction

One bishop, one Eucharist celebrated, one place where that Eucharist is celebrated. If the Orthodox answer to the question "what is the Church?" is based on the Eucharist and the episcopacy, it is above all because Orthodox ecclesiology recognizes the local community as the fundamental unit of its structure, in which the fullness of the Church is represented. A "diocese" is the administrative structure placed under the authority of a bishop, while each "local Church" is made up of a set of dioceses. For example, all of the Orthodox dioceses of Romania form the Patriarchate of Romania. The gathering of all the bishops of a local Church forms a synod.

Conciliarity

What happens when bishops are gathered? Councils, particularly ecumenical councils, are the best illustration of conciliarity, the other organizational pillar of the Orthodox Church. Conciliarity, also known as synodality, reflects the Eucharistic assembly, manifesting the hierarchs' consensus on questions of both faith and organization. For example, more than three hundred bishops from Asia Minor, Palestine, Egypt, and the West gathered at the First Ecumenical Council, held at Nicaea in 325, where they affirmed the reality of Christ's divinity and rejected the teachings of Arius.

However, bishops are not entirely autonomous in their decision-making. While a council is a visible manifestation of synodality, it only acquires real authority once it has been received by the clergy and the people who make up the body of the Church. The rejection of the Council of Ferrara-Florence (1438-1439) is a very clear example of the weight of this ecclesial conscience. Most of the bishops who had attended the council later recanted when they encountered the opposition of their faithful.

In addition to their tremendous importance in defining the faith, the ecumenical councils have also strongly influenced the organization of the Church. The conciliar experience produced the institutional model that the Orthodox Church continues to apply today, known as autocephaly, and, by extension, defined the concept of primacy.

The pentarchy

Gatherings like liturgies, synods, and councils created a need to organize and structure the Christian community around a leader. Eucharistic typology was a component of this development process. As the administrative structure of the Church developed, the act of presiding over the Eucharist (*proestos*) both determined and manifested synodal leadership. The emergence of a Pentarchy of the five historic patriarchates (in order of precedence: Rome, Constantinople, Alexandria, Antioch and Jerusalem) came to form the organizational and canonical basis of the Orthodox Church, in line with the decisions of the ecumenical councils, particularly the council of Chalcedon (451). Each patriarchate is made up of dioceses that are headed by bishops, archbishops, or metropolitans. The seats of four of the ancient Patriarchates correspond to the leading cities of the Roman Empire; Jerusalem is the fifth due to its unique connection with the events of the life of Christ.

The Byzantine tradition has always been strongly attached to this structure. The Pentarchy, which was common to East and West until 1054, was shaken by the schism with Rome. Even today, however, the Orthodox Church continues to recognize that Rome holds a form of primacy of honor, although it does not accept its claims to universal prerogatives.

The Pentarchy ultimately became the model for local autocephaly – the existence of independent churches – in the Orthodox Church. After Cyprus, which was recognized as an autocephalous church at the third Ecumenical Council (Ephesus, 431), a whole series of autocephalous churches were recognized in quick succession in the lands evangelized by Byzantine missionaries in the ninth century. Later, hundreds of years under the Ottoman yoke left the Orthodox Church highly centralized around the Patriarchate of Constantinople. During the same period, the Russian Church was subjected to the Russian State, a situation best illustrated by the replacement of the Patriarchate with a synodal system in 1721 by Peter the Great as part of his efforts to mold a servile Church. The end of the nineteenth century saw a strong revival of autocephaly in a very different context. The rise of nationalism in the Balkans revealed that the dream of the nation-state also meant an autocephalous church. The successive proclamations of the autocephaly of the Churches of Serbia (1879), Romania (1885), and many more were symptomatic of the fusion of religious and national identity.

The patriarchal model

The current organization of the Orthodox Church is based on the historic patriarchates, its mission, and the changes that have shaped the modern world. The Church is organized on several distinct levels.

The autocephalous churches

The autocephalous churches were formed from the ancient patriarchates. They are characterized by equal dignity, territorial boundaries, and a form of administration or independence expressed through the sovereign election of their primate. The autocephalous Orthodox churches are:

- The Ecumenical Patriarchate of Constantinople (headquartered in Istanbul, and holding primacy in lieu of Rome);
- The Patriarchate of Alexandria and All Africa (with the title of Pope);
- The Patriarchate of Antioch and all the East (headquartered in Damascus);
- The Patriarchate of Jerusalem and all Palestine;
- The Patriarchate of Moscow and all Russia;
- The Patriarchate of Georgia (with the title of Catholicos);
- The Patriarchate of Serbia (with the title of Patriarch);
- The Patriarchate of Romania (with the title of Patriarch);
- The Patriarchate of Bulgaria (with the title of Patriarch);
- The Church of Cyprus (with the title of Archbishop);
- The Church of Greece (with the title of Archbishop);
- The Church of Albania (with the title of Archbishop);

- The Church of Poland (with the title of Metropolitan);
- The Orthodox Church of the Czech Lands and Slovakia (headquartered in Presov, with the title of Metropolitan);
- The Orthodox Church in Ukraine (its autocephaly was granted by the Ecumenical Patriarchate in 2019, but is not recognized by all the Orthodox Churches).

The Orthodox Church in America was granted autocephaly by the Patriarchate of Moscow in 1970 but is not recognized as such by the Ecumenical Patriarchate and some other Churches. Eucharistic communion with the Macedonian Orthodox Church – Archdiocese of Ohrid was reestablished in 2022.

The Autonomous Churches

The autonomous Churches manage their own internal affairs but depend on an autocephalous Church. These Churches include:

- The Church of Sinai at the Monastery of Saint Catherine (under the jurisdiction of the Patriarchate of Jerusalem);
- The Church of Finland, (under the jurisdiction of the Ecumenical Patriarchate);
- The Churches of Japan, Belarus, Moldova, and Latvia (under the jurisdiction of the Patriarchate of Moscow).

Geopolitics of Orthodoxy

A heterogeneous reality

On a geopolitical level, the Orthodox Church is not the homogeneous block of some observers' imaginations but a highly complex reality. The rise of irredentism over the course of the nineteenth century set the stage for a process of territorial fragmentation that continued throughout the twentieth century. As a series of historical events shrank the homelands of Orthodox communities, they were pushed to seek refuge in the West, redrawing the global map of Orthodoxy. These events included the Russian Revolution (1917), the population exchange between Greece and Türkiye (1923), the Ustache massacres

(1942-1944), the rise of Communism in the Balkans (1945), tensions in the Middle East (starting in 1948), the invasion and partition of Cyprus (1974), the Lebanese civil war (1975), the Balkan wars (1991-2000), the fall of the Soviet Union (1991), the US-led military intervention in Iraq (2003), the independence of Kosovo (2008), the Russo-Georgian War (2008), the Arab Spring (2010), the Syrian crisis (2011), and more recently, the conflict in Ukraine (since 2014) and the ongoing Russian invasion (2022).

Today, Orthodox unity appears to be endangered by a geopolitical context that weighs on the relationship between faith and politics. The Orthodox Church has responded to the dramatic changes of the past century by developing approaches that focus on the dialogue between Orthodoxy and identity and address both the ways that territorial changes have affected the local churches' strategy for preserving spiritual authority in diaspora communities and in some cases their role in armed conflicts.

International influence

The Orthodox population continues to grow worldwide. However, it is decreasing as a share of the global population due to its relatively low growth rate. According to Antoine Arjakovsky: "The Orthodox population doubled over the course of the twentieth century [...] from 124,923,000 to 274,447,000 in 2010."[17] The convergence of territorial fragmentation and population growth has brought Orthodoxy back onto the global stage while simultaneously producing a profound shift in outlook among all fourteen autocephalous churches.

In the twentieth century, Orthodoxy became a major and influential global presence. In the wake of the Cold War and 9/11, the local Orthodox Churches implemented their own strategies to thrive and grow in their traditional homelands and worldwide. Often defensive, these approaches have generally been linked to the process of ethno-religious fusion that continues to fuel nationalism in southeastern Europe and Russia. At the same time, the center of gravity of Orthodoxy is moving outside its traditional borders, leading to new geopolitical realities and new alliances in increasingly secular societies.

---
17 Arjakovsky, Antoine, *Qu'est-ce que l'orthodoxie* (Gallimard, 2013).

Nationalism and the Orthodox Church

Nationalism in the Orthodox Church is the result of the fusion of ethnic and religious identity that began in the nineteenth century under Ottoman domination. As the symbol of the identity of a minority community, Orthodoxy became the bedrock of modern nationalism in many Balkan nations, where it was combined with separatist projects that redrew the political map of southeastern Europe. The process of nation-building was accompanied by church-building. Separatist demands were met with the autocephalies granted to the Churches of Greece (1833), Serbia (1832), the Exarchate of Bulgaria (1870), Romania (1885), and more. The fusion of ethnic and religious identity laid the groundwork for the emergence of national Churches. The definition of a religious identity based on ethnicity was not limited to the old country. In the diaspora, parallel parish communities formed as successive waves of immigrants from different Orthodox regions reached new lands. The merger of ethnic and religious identity, also known as ethnophyletism, was officially condemned in 1872 at the Council of Constantinople. Despite its official condemnation, the ethnonational paradigm still remains deeply anchored in the life and organization of the Orthodox Church today. Its primary modern expression is the subjection of the Church to the political authorities to varying degrees in different places.

Fundamentalism

In addition to the challenge of nationalism, Orthodoxy is experiencing a surge in fundamentalism or ultra-conservatism, characterized by its opposition to modernity, liberalism, development of church practice, and inter-Christian and interfaith dialogues. It idealizes history and sacralizes the past in an attempt to establish sources of authority and authenticity within the Church that are independent of the hierarchy. Beyond mere theological positions, Orthodox fundamentalism over-emphasizes the purity of moral and traditional values, often avoiding a spirit of dialogue and compassion. This fundamentalism has established a new hierarchy of authority and authenticity, drawing from a selective reading of the Holy Fathers, the Saints, canonical tradition, and modern spiritual leaders or "elders" (*gerontes* or *startsi*), to defend the Orthodox faith against perceived internal and external challenges. Often used for political leverage, Orthodox fundamentalism has fostered opposition that threatens Orthodox unity, a trend that is particularly evident in the digital sphere. In terms of social issues, it tends to prioritize strict adherence to doctrine and practice over economy, in the theological sense of pastoral care.

Various other political agendas and the growth of diaspora communities are powerful forces that are reshaping interorthodox relations today. The war in Ukraine and the continuing crisis in Syria are particularly emblematic of the major geopolitical challenges facing Orthodoxy as it enters its third millennium.

Other ongoing geopolitical issues include:

- The official recognition of the legal status of the Ecumenical Patriarchate by the Turkish government, as well as the reopening of the seminary in Halki;
- Protection for Middle Eastern Christians;
- The compatibility of the Russian Orthodox Church and the West;
- The EU membership process in Serbia and the treatment of the Orthodox Church in Kosovo;
- The role of the Orthodox Church in Greece in a time of economic and migration crises;
- The continued division of Cyprus;
- The break in communion between the Patriarchates of Moscow and Constantinople over the situation in Ukraine.

Threats and revival

In the East, the Patriarchates of Constantinople, Antioch, and Jerusalem are threatened by the exodus of local Christians and depend on their diasporas to survive, while the Patriarchate of Alexandria is experiencing impressive growth in Africa despite the recent incursion of the Moscow Patriarchate on the continent. In post-communist Europe, the catholicosate of Tbilisi (Georgia) is suffering from regional instability in the Caucasus. The Patriarchate of Serbia is seriously affected by Serbia's political marginalization and is prevented from ministering to its historic communities in Kosovo. The Church of Albania is experiencing a remarkable revival. In Western Europe, the Church of Greece, long the only Orthodox Church in the European Union, was joined by the Churches of Cyprus, Poland, and the Czech and Slovak lands in 2004 and by the Patriarchates of Romania and Bulgaria in 2007. The risk of rapid secularization that comes with European integration is offset by strong popular piety, particularly in Greece and Romania.

Beyond its purely institutional aspects, the life and existence of the Orthodox Church are dominated by the revival of the monastic republic of Mount Athos and by the spirit of dialogue that marked twentieth century theology. The Orthodox commitment to dialogue underscores the fact that, as long as Orthodoxy rejects the logic of the clash of civilizations, it remains an essential intermediary between East and West.

This list is far from exhaustive, but it does highlight the difficulty faced by the Orthodox Church in strengthening its organic unity as a communion of Churches. Throughout the twentieth century, the Orthodox Church showed remarkable flexibility in adapting to different political situations, from Greece, where it is the state religion, to countries like Russia and Albania, where it suffered brutal communist persecution.

| The Holy and Great Council (2016)

The Holy and Great Council of the Orthodox Church, which was held in Crete in June 2016 under the leadership of His All-Holiness Ecumenical Patriarch Bartholomew, was by far one of the most important events in twenty-first century Orthodoxy. The council crystallized many of the contemporary challenges facing the Orthodox Church. While some observers have compared it to Vatican II (1962-1965) for Catholicism, the conciliar nature of the Orthodox Church made the Holy and Great Council a very different event, despite its equally historic weight.

Chronology of the conciliar process

- **1961:** First Pan-Orthodox Meeting, Rhodes
- **1962:** Second Pan-Orthodox Meeting, Rhodes
- **1963:** Third Pan-Orthodox Meeting, Rhodes
- **1968:** Fourth Pan-Orthodox Meeting, Chambésy
- **1971:** Inter-Orthodox Preparatory Commission, Chambésy
- **1976:** First Pre-Conciliar Pan-Orthodox Conference, Chambésy (topics covered: methodology, relationships with other Christian churches, and common celebration of Easter)
- **1982:** Second Pre-Conciliar Pan-Orthodox Conference, Chambésy (topics covered: impediments to marriage and fasting rules)
- **1986:** Third Pre-Conciliar Pan-Orthodox Conference, Chambésy (topics covered: fasting rules, the mission of the Orthodox Church in the world)
- **1992:** First Synaxis (meeting) of the Primates of Orthodox Churches, Istanbul
- **1995:** Second Synaxis of the Primates of Orthodox Churches, Patmos
- **2000:** Third Synaxis of the Primates of Orthodox Churches, Jerusalem, Bethlehem, Istanbul, and Nicaea
- **2008:** Fourth Synaxis of the Primates of Orthodox Churches, Istanbul
- **2009:** Fourth Pre-Conciliar Pan-Orthodox Conference, Chambésy (topic covered: assemblies of bishops in the diaspora)
- **2014:** Fifth Synaxis of the Primates of Orthodox Churches, Istanbul
- **2015:** Fifth Pre-Conciliar Pan-Orthodox Conference, Chambésy
- **2016:** Sixth Synaxis of the Primates of Orthodox Churches, Chambésy
- **June 16-27, 2016:** The Holy and Great Council of the Orthodox Church

A historic process

The historic process that led up to the Holy and Great Council began in the early twentieth century. In 1902, Ecumenical Patriarch Joachim III (1834-1912) issued an encyclical calling on the different Orthodox Churches to increase their collaboration in response to the challenges of the time, particularly nationalism and the new autocephalous churches that had emerged in response to irredentism in the new Balkan nation-states. After World War I, Ecumenical Patriarch Photius II (1874-1935) convened the first inter-Orthodox committee, which met on Mount Athos at the monastery of Vatopedi in 1930. The idea of a council first appeared at this meeting but was quickly shelved due to the outbreak of World War II.

It returned to the fore in the 1950s with Ecumenical Patriarch Athenagoras (1886-1972). In the 1960s, a series of pan-Orthodox meetings was held in Rhodes (Greece). During these meetings, an initial list of the topics to be discussed during the council was drawn up. Ten topics were ultimately selected and a document on each one was prepared during the series of pre-conciliar pan-Orthodox conferences, which started in 1976 and ended in October 2015 with the meeting that approved and finalized the last documents to be submitted to the council. Four months later, in January 2016, the fourteen primates of the local Orthodox Churches met to finalize the council's agenda. The Holy and Great Council was given six texts on which to work:

1. The Mission of the Orthodox Church in Today's World
2. The Orthodox Diaspora
3. Autonomy and the Means by Which it is Proclaimed
4. The Sacrament of Marriage and its Impediments
5. The Importance of Fasting and Its Observance Today
6. Relations of the Orthodox Church with the Rest of the Christian World

Organizational challenges

The Holy and Great Council, which was originally intended to be held in Istanbul, was ultimately scheduled for June 18 to 27, 2016 at the Orthodox Academy of Crete (Greece) due to the conflicts in the Middle East and rising tensions between the governments of Russia and Türkiye. The conciliar process was undermined by last-minute drama when the Patriarchates of Antioch, Bulgaria, Georgia, and Moscow decided not to attend for different reasons.

Bulgaria was the first to make its announcement, following a series of signals that suggested it might pull out of the event. On June 1, 2016, the Holy Synod of the Church of Bulgaria had requested the postponement of the Holy and Great Council due to a large number of open questions, particularly the incomplete agenda. The document also discussed the hierarchs' seating arrangements; the Synod argued that the plan to seat them in an arc formation would violate their equality. The Church of Bulgaria remains one of the most isolated Orthodox Churches in Europe.

Antioch's objections were also foreseeable, despite the Ecumenical Patriarchate's attempts at mediation between Antioch and Jerusalem regarding who has jurisdiction over Qatar. In a statement dated June 6, the Holy Synod of the Patriarchate of Antioch officially canceled its participation in the Council, asking that it be adjourned until its dispute with the Patriarchate of Jerusalem over Qatar was fully resolved.

On June 13, the Patriarchate of Moscow announced that it, too, would back out of the Council due to the absence of other Churches. This decision, which was made by the top leadership within the Russian Church, was a departure from its previous highly favorable stance on the Council. Many observers have connected Moscow's apparent openness following Patriarch Kirill's February 2016 meeting with Pope Francis in Cuba to its affirmation of its commitment to participating in pan-Orthodox projects. By refusing to attend the Council, the Russian Church marked both its opposition to the Ecumenical Patriarchate and the formation of a Slavic Orthodox nexus.

On the same day, the Patriarchate of Georgia sent Ecumenical Patriarch Bartholomew a letter notifying him of the decision of its Holy Synod not to send its delegation to the council. During the January 2016 synaxis of primates in Chambésy (Switzerland), Patriarch Ilia had already expressed fierce opposition to the document on Orthodox relations with the rest of the Christian world.

Despite all these conflicts, the Holy and Great Council did ultimately take place thanks to the determination of Ecumenical Patriarch Batholomew, who put tremendous energy into saving the conciliar process in the final days leading up to its opening. The Council met in a reduced format, with just ten of the autocephalous Orthodox Churches in attendance. The delegations, each made up of twenty-four bishops, were led by the primates of their churches. More than one hundred and fifty bishops attended the Council, the first of its kind to be held by the Orthodox Church in over twelve hundred years, since before the Great Schism of 1054. In many ways, it marked Orthodoxy's return to history after a twentieth century in which it struggled under the burdens of persecution, atheism, exile, and war, some of which continue today, particularly in the Middle East and Ukraine.

| The Balkanization of Orthodoxy

The balkanization of Orthodoxy today is largely due to the revival of a national focus that often verges on nationalism, a trend highlighted by the withdrawal of four patriarchates from the conciliar process. Events moved fast in the weeks leading up to the Council, due to both the growing opposition to the Council itself in the most conservative factions of the local Churches and the systemic effects of the structure of the Orthodox Church. All of the Holy Synods (decision-making bodies made up of the bishops of the local Churches and chaired by their primates) of the local Orthodox Churches met before the opening of the Holy and Great Council to discuss the preconciliar documents and determine who would join the delegations accompanying the primates. It quickly became clear that the most controversial documents were the ones on the mission of the Church in today's world and the relations of the Orthodox Church with the rest of the Christian world. The debate centered on the use of the word "Church" for non-Orthodox Christian communities (the Roman Catholic Church and Protestant Churches). This issue was raised by the Churches of Bulgaria, Georgia, and Greece, as well as in a letter from Mount Athos. Ecumenism has been and remains an extremely precise indicator of the different Churches' levels of isolation.

Despite the absence of four local churches, the Holy and Great Council was a key event for contemporary Orthodoxy. In addition to the six documents on which the Council fathers reached an agreement, the Council produced two supplemental documents: an Encyclical and a Message. For Ecumenical Patriarch Bartholomew, this experience, difficult as it was, constituted the starting point for a profound renewal of the principle of collegiality and consensus on which the experience of communion that has defined Orthodoxy over the centuries is based. The Message of the Council concludes with the words,

> *The Holy and Great Council has opened our horizon towards the contemporary diverse and multifarious world. It has emphasized our responsibility in place and in time, ever with the perspective of eternity. The Orthodox Church, preserving intact her Sacramental and Soteriological character, is sensitive to the pain, the distress and the cry for justice and peace of the peoples of the world.*[18]

(Para. 12.)

| Key points

- The Orthodox Church is a diverse communion of fifteen autocephalous Churches. It is one because it is united to the Universal Church through the celebration of the Eucharist. The figure of the bishop plays a key role in establishing the tie of communion on which the institution and organization of Orthodoxy are based.

---

18 All the documents of the Holy and Great Council are available in English at www.holycouncil.org.

- The Orthodox Churches are also geopolitical realities with state ties that reflect the different ways in which religion can be fused with national identity.

- The Holy and Great Council of the Orthodox Church in June 2016 sought to address the power struggles between the Churches by building a spirit of conciliarity among the autocephalous churches. The absence of four Churches at the Council reveals how crucial the question of unity is for Orthodoxy today.

PART 3
Orthodox Worship

| Chapter 7
| Orthodox Worship

In this chapter

- Liturgy
- Sacraments
- Feast days, prayer, and fasting

In the words of Evagrius Ponticus (345-399), "only those who pray are theologians." Orthodoxy also means orthopraxy. In Orthodox theology, faith is inseparable from the actions that authenticate it. Prayer (*lex orandi*) confirms doctrine (*lex credendi*) and vice versa. Liturgy, both communal and personal, is primordial in the Orthodox Church. The word "liturgy" refers to different forms of celebration and contemplation. The Eucharist, other religious services, the calendar and feasts, and personal prayer are all "liturgies." Through them, the baptized people of God live out their priestly vocation.[19]

---

[19] Cf. Schmemann, Alexander, *For the Life of the World – New Edition* (St. Vladimir's Seminary Press, 2018)

Liturgy embodies Orthodox identity and continuity. The expressions of its theology are not only confessions of faith: they are acts of praise.

| Liturgy

The Byzantine rite includes several Eucharistic liturgies, known as "Divine Liturgies," all of which show strong semitic influence from their Syriac roots. The liturgies used in the life of the Church are, in order of frequency of use, the liturgies attributed to Saint John Chrysostom, Saint Basil the Great (fourth century), and Saint James, the Brother of the Lord (usually offered only annually on his feast day, October 23). During Great Lent, when the Divine Liturgy is celebrated only on Saturdays, Sundays, and certain feast days (e.g. Annunciation, March 25), the "liturgy of the presanctified gifts," a vespers service with holy communion that is attributed to Pope Gregory the Great (590-604), is celebrated on weekdays. The Divine Liturgy is both a mystical drama that reproduces heavenly worship on Earth and a revelation of the last things. It is the commemoration of the Mystical Supper and a manifestation of the Kingdom. The words of Christ are brought into the present during the *epiclesis*, the prayer for the descent of the Holy Spirit, the fervor of which highlights the sacramental realism of Orthodoxy.

The "Liturgy of the Hours" provides the framework for the Eucharist. The services of matins, vespers, and compline, which were developed in monasteries, also mark out the rhythm of parish life. The different worship services also offer religious education for the faithful. The daily, weekly, annual, and Paschal cycles and feast days are marked by profoundly theological Byzantine hymns. These hymns recapitulate the Scriptures and Church History and incorporate biblical and Greek poetry, catechizing the faithful as they worship. Two of the best-known composers of Orthodox religious music are the theologians Saints Romanos the Melodist (490-556) and Theodore the Studite (759-826).[20]

---

[20] Cf. Getcha, Job, *The Typikon Decoded: An Explanation of Byzantine Liturgical Practice* (St. Vladimir's Seminary Press, 2012).

Finally, the liturgy also has a cosmic meaning. Orthodox churches are built according to strict architectural and artistic guidelines, echoing the symbolism of the Old Testament temple. The iconostasis, a screen decorated with icons, separates the Holy of Holies, which is reserved for those serving in the altar, from the nave where the faithful pray. The iconostasis is not so much a veil as a transparent window into a transfigured universe. With its gold and incense, the intricate movements of the clergy, sacred music, blessings of water, veneration of the Cross and icons, anointings with oil, consumption of boiled wheat kernels in memory of the dead, standing and prostrations, the Orthodox liturgy is a highly physical experience. That physicality reflects the sanctification of the flesh through the incarnation. The sanctification of the whole world is also why Pascha, or Easter, is the "feast of feasts:" the joyous and luminous day that celebrates the resurrection of Christ as the entry of a world made new into God's glory.

| The Sacraments

The Orthodox understanding of sacraments is not limited to the seven fundamental actions of baptism, chrismation, the Eucharist, marriage, ordination, confession, and unction. It extends to all forms of supplication, intercession, and offering, including funerals and monastic tonsuring, and incorporates every aspect of life. The sacraments are deeply personal: the names of the faithful receiving the sacrament are extremely important in the prayers read by the priest, through which the grace of God is made manifest in the Church. The texts of the sacraments are compiled in a book called the *euchologion* (*trebnik* in the Slavic churches).

| Baptism and chrismation

All three sacraments of Christian initiation (baptism, chrismation, and communion) are given together, and can be administered from birth.

The sacrament of baptism comprises the invocation of the name of the Trinity (Father, Son, and Holy Spirit) and a triple immersion. The priest pronounces the prayer: "The servant of God (name) is baptized in the name of the Father and of the Son and of the Holy Spirit, Amen!" while immersing the person being baptized three times in the water. This triple immersion recalls Christ's three days in the tomb before His resurrection, linking Baptism to the paschal mystery of the resurrection. In keeping with the ancient practice, Orthodox baptisms are generally performed by full immersion. Baptism absolves the newly baptized Christian of all previous sins and sets him or her on the path towards the kingdom of God.

After being baptized by triple immersion and confirmed with the Holy Chrism (chrismation) in the name of the Holy Spirit, the new member of the Church is immediately allowed to receive the Eucharist. These three sacraments are so intimately linked as to be inseparable.

> *It is the Sacraments that constitute the life in Christ.*
>
> Saint Nicholas Cabasilas (fourteenth century)

Eucharistic Communion and the Divine Liturgy

Eucharistic Communion is administered in both species, the bread and the wine. Unlike the unleavened hosts used in the Roman Catholic tradition, the Orthodox Church uses leavened bread as a symbol of Christ's glorified humanity because the consecration of the gifts is inseparable from the consecration of those who receive them.

The Eucharist, which in Greek means "thanksgiving," can be celebrated in four ways.

- The Divine Liturgy of Saint John Chrysostom, the most common.
- The Divine Liturgy of Saint Basil the Great, celebrated about ten times every year, mainly during Great Lent.
- The Divine Liturgy of Saint James, the Brother of the Lord, which is celebrated just once a year on October 23, the feast of Saint James.
- The Liturgy of Presanctified Gifts, celebrated only on Wednesdays and Fridays during Great Lent, the period of fasting before

Pascha (Easter). The Liturgy of the Presanctified Gifts is only a communion service; the Eucharist distributed was consecrated during the Divine Liturgy on the previous Sunday.

The Divine Liturgy is divided into three parts:

- The preparation, also known as the *prothesis* or *proskomidia*, during which the bread and the wine are prepared for consecration.
- The liturgy of the word, during which the Gospel and Epistle are read and preached.
- The Eucharist itself, during which the Creed of Nicaea-Constantinople (325-381) and the Eucharistic prayers (*anamnesis, epiclesis*, consecration, and communion) are read and the Eucharist is distributed. The Divine Liturgy ends with prayers of thanksgiving and the distribution of blessed bread called *antidoron*.

The Eucharist is central to the life of Orthodox Christians because Orthodoxy teaches that the bread and wine become the body and blood of Christ after the consecration. This change, while it remains an unexplained mystery, makes Christ a real presence on the altar. It is not only a remembrance (*anamnesis*) of the event of the Mystical Supper but a sacrifice understood as identical to the sacrifice of the Cross. The bread and the wine are offered to God when they are elevated by the celebrant (*anaphora*) before he prays for the descent of the Holy Spirit (*epiclesis*):

> *Once again we offer to You this spiritual worship without the shedding of blood, and we beseech and pray and entreat you: Send down Your Holy Spirit upon us and upon the gifts here presented...*
>
> Divine Liturgy of Saint John Chrysostom

Orthodox Christians are expected to fast from eating and drinking from midnight before receiving Communion. The frequency of communion depends on the local practice of each Church. The sacrament of confession may be required as preparation for Communion.

Confession

The sacrament of confession or penitence (in Greek, *exomologesis* or *metanoia*) absolves sins committed after baptism, granting the penitent forgiveness and reconciling him or her with the Church. Confession should not be understood in the legal terms often used to describe it in the West. In the Orthodox understanding, confession is a therapeutic act that purifies the soul of the evil passions that separate it from God. The priest is first and foremost a witness to the repentance of those who come to confession. He is bound by the secrecy of confession and does not grant absolution in his own name but reminds the penitent that it is God Himself who forgives sin. The priest may also offer spiritual advice. While confession was public in the early Church, it gradually became a private conversation between the priest and the penitent. At the end of the confession, the priest covers the penitent's head with his stole (*epitrachelion*) and recites the prayer of absolution.

The priest can also, when he considers it appropriate, impose a penance (*epitimion*) to help anchor the repentance in the penitent's heart. Orthodox Christians do not necessarily go to their own parish priest for confession. They often have a "spiritual father" who guides their religious life, particularly through the sacrament of confession. The frequency of confession depends on the customs of each local Church.

> *Have you sinned? Enter the church, confess and your sins will be erased. Repent any time you sin. If you sin again, repent again, and never lose hope, for the church is a hospital and not a court, for He does not condemn us for our sins.*
>
> Saint John Chrysostom

Ordination

All of the sacraments depend on the sacrament of Ordination, or Holy Orders. The Orthodox Church recognizes three major orders: deacons, priests, and bishops. It also has two minor orders: sub-deacons and readers.

All three of the major orders are ordained during the Divine Liturgy. Only bishops have the authority to ordain by the laying on of hands. To demonstrate the conciliar nature of the Church, which the bishop represents as a successor of the apostles, bishops are ordained by the laying on of the Gospels by at least three other bishops and acclaimed by the people. Bishops have been required to be monks since the sixth century. Priests and deacons must be married or monks prior to ordination; married clergy may only be married once. Because the grace of the priesthood can operate only within the assembly that legitimates it, Orthodox priests cannot celebrate the Eucharist alone. Lay members of the Church are also involved in the ordination service: they express their consent by shouting "*Axios*" ("he is worthy"). Today, there are increasing numbers of celibate priests who have not been tonsured as monks.

Only men are ordained to the three major orders. Ancient tradition, however, allowed the ordination of women as deaconesses. While this practice fell out of use centuries ago, there are now intense debates about its potential revival.

> *For the Priest ought not only to be thus pure as one who has been dignified with so high a ministry, but very discreet, and skilled in many matters, and to be as well versed in the affairs of this life as they who are engaged in the world, and yet to be free from them all more than the recluses who occupy the mountains.*
>
> Saint John Chrysostom

| Marriage

The sacrament of marriage celebrates the union in the Church of a man and a woman, based on the mystery of unity at the heart of the Trinity. The image of God in human beings calls us to a relational vocation of communion in which the fruit of love forms a family. Marriage is placed under God's protection and blessing and is considered a vocation, on an equal footing with the monastic vocation.

The marriage service comprises two parts: the betrothal and the crowning. The crowning is the actual sacrament of marriage.

During the betrothal service, the couple's rings are exchanged. In the Orthodox Church, the bride and groom generally do not recite vows. During the second part of the ceremony, crowns are placed on their heads as a visible symbol of the grace of the Holy Spirit that unites them. The bride and groom then drink from a common cup of wine as a symbol of the common life that they are called to share.

Orthodoxy recognizes that marriages can fail and allows divorce and remarriage, with a strict lifetime limit of three marriages. Its tolerance of divorce does not negate the ideal of a single marriage. It is a pastoral response to human weakness that seeks to help the faithful overcome their past failures and bring them to salvation.[21]

The Orthodox Church teaches that sexual relations are for marriage. In Orthodox teaching, the profound purpose of sexuality is not merely reproduction but deepening the love that unites the couple. Orthodoxy also teaches that marriage is chaste and equal in dignity to the monastic life and that its purpose cannot be reduced to procreation. This profound respect for the marriage relationship explains why the Orthodox Church does not regulate the intimate marital life of the faithful. The acceptability of contraception depends mainly on the methods used, which must not be abortifacient. The Orthodox Church very clearly condemns abortion, in the name of the protection of human life. However, it does encourage a pastoral approach to these sensitive issues.

The Orthodox Church allows marriages between an Orthodox Christian and a Christian of another confession. However, interreligious couples cannot receive the sacrament of marriage.

> The union of man and woman in Christ constitutes "a small church" or an icon of the Church. Through God's blessing, the union of man and woman is elevated to a higher level, for communion is greater than individual existence because it initiates the spouses into the order of the Kingdom of the All-Holy Trinity. A necessary condition

---

21 Cf. Meyendorff, John, *Marriage: on Orthodox Perspective* (St. Vladimir's Seminary Press, 1975)

of marriage is faith in Jesus Christ, which must be shared by the bridegroom and the bride, man and woman. Consequently, unity in Christ is the foundation of marital unity. Thus, marital love blessed by the Holy Spirit enables the couple to reflect the love between Christ and the Church as a mystery of the Kingdom of God – as the eternal life of humanity in the love of God.

Holy and Great Council, 2016

Holy Unction

Are any among you sick? They should call for the elders of the church and have them pray over them, anointing them with oil in the name of the Lord. The prayer of faith will save the sick, and the Lord will raise them up, and anyone who has committed sins will be forgiven. Therefore confess your sins to one another and pray for one another, so that you may be healed. The prayer of the righteous is powerful and effective.

James 5:13-16

Holy unction, the sacrament of the "oil of prayer," is offered for the healing of the soul and body. This sacrament reflects a holistic understanding of the human person. It is not a form of magic. Even if the person is not immediately cured, the grace received through the sacrament will help them to bear or accept their sickness or even death. Holy unction can be celebrated at the request of the person in need or their loved ones and is also traditionally celebrated on the evening of Holy Wednesday.

Holy unction can also be administered in preparation for death. The hope that lies at the heart of Orthodoxy is clearly expressed in the liturgy for the dying. Traditionally, the Psalms are read as an Orthodox Christian is dying and over their body after death. Funerals are open casket and the service continues at the cemetery for the internment. Memorial services are held on the third, ninth, and fortieth days after death, and then annually on the anniversary. When Orthodox Christians die during the Paschal season, a special funeral service that is an explicit celebration of the resurrection is used instead of the usual, far more mournful funeral. All of humanity, living and dead, is united in the expectation of Christ's return. The familiarity with the invisible that is characteristic of Orthodoxy extends to the company of the saints.[22]

Feast days, prayer, and fasting

The twelve great feasts

The Orthodox Church celebrates twelve major feasts that commemorate events in the lives of Christ and His mother, the Virgin Mary. These twelve feasts are organized in two liturgical cycles. The fixed cycle includes all the feasts that fall on the same set date every year: the Nativity of the Most Holy Mother of God (September 8), the Exaltation of the Most Holy Cross (September 14), the Presentation of the Most Holy Mother of God in the Temple (November 21), the Nativity of Christ (December 25), the Baptism of Christ, better known as Theophany (January 6), the Presentation of Christ in the Temple (February 2), the Annunciation (March 25), the Transfiguration (August 6), and the Dormition of the Mother of God (August 15). The movable cycle is centered around the feast of Pascha, or Easter, which commemorates Christ's resurrection. Pascha is the greatest feast of the Orthodox Church. It is not numbered among the twelve major feasts because it is considered the "Feast of Feasts," thus greater than all the others. The other feasts on the movable cycle are Palm Sunday (one week before Pascha), Ascension (forty days before Pascha), and Pentecost (fifty days after Pascha).

Certain feasts are marked by special services and prayers:

- The blessing of the waters on Theophany
- The blessing of the grapes on the Transfiguration
- The procession and veneration of the Cross on the Elevation of the Holy Cross

---

22 Breck, John, *The Sacred Gift of Life* (St. Vladimir's Seminary Press, 1998)

- Kneeling Vespers on Pentecost,
- The procession with the *epitaphios* (representation of Christ in the tomb) on the evening of Holy Friday.

All of these moments share a particular intensity that culminates on Pascha with the celebration of Christ's resurrection.

The liturgical calendar

The Orthodox liturgical year starts on September 1. Some Orthodox Churches follow the Julian Calendar, popularly known as the Old Calendar (13 days behind the civil calendar), while others have adopted the Gregorian calendar. For example, Christmas is celebrated on December 25 on the Gregorian calendar, while on the Old Calendar it is celebrated thirteen days later, on January 7. With a very few exceptions, all Orthodox Churches celebrate Pascha on the same date. The date of Pascha is still calculated based on the Julian calendar, using a formula developed during the First Ecumenical Council. That is why Orthodox Pascha only rarely coincides with Catholic and Protestant Easter. The use of the Gregorian calendar for the fixed cycle and the Julian calendar for the movable cycle is also known as the "revised Julian Calendar" or "New Calendar."

Prayer and fasting

Personal prayer occupies a central place in Orthodox life since it opens and closes each day. Prayer books are available for personal daily prayer. They contain many of the prayers read in church, highlighting the continuity between personal and liturgical life. They also include prayers of preparation for Communion. In addition to these prayers, the recitation of the Jesus prayer, anytime and anywhere, is a key part of Orthodox spirituality.

Orthodox Christians offer prayers for the dead, showing that there is no impenetrable barrier between the living and the dead. Christ's resurrection has bridged the gap between life and death. Orthodoxy does not adhere to the Catholic doctrine of purgatory, instead accepting that the condition of souls after death is a mystery, although its prayers for the dead are supplications for their communion with God's infinite holiness.

The Orthodox Church practices food fasting. In the Orthodox tradition, fasting means abstaining from all animal products (meat, eggs, milk, fish other than shellfish, etc.) and even certain plant-based products (oil and wine) during strict fasts. There are four annual fasting periods and most Wednesdays and Fridays throughout the year are also fast days. The most important fast is Great Lent, the forty days leading up to Pascha. It is followed by the Apostles' Fast, which starts one week after Pentecost and ends on the feast of the Apostles Peter and Paul, on June 29. The first two weeks of August are the Dormition Fast. Finally, the forty days before Christmas make up the Nativity Fast.

The Orthodox Church does not have any specific dress requirements. However, women may be asked to cover their heads in some churches and monasteries as a sign of respect for the sacredness of the space. This practice varies culturally.

> *The annual liturgical cycle reflects the entire patristic teaching on fasting, the teaching on constant and unceasing watchfulness of the human person, and our participation in spiritual struggles.*
>
> Holy and Great Council, 2016

| Key points

- Orthodoxy is deeply attached to its liturgy. Its worship and spirituality are the most tangible expression of its eastern identity. The Church is manifested in and through the liturgy. The liturgy is the common work that is the foundation of the tie of communion that unites all the members of the Church. The liturgy is a bridge between the visible and the invisible, making all baptized Christians participants in the union of the human and the divine that is accomplished in Christ.

- While Orthodoxy does not limit itself to a list of seven sacraments, it recognizes the importance of certain rites through which the faithful can participate in the mystery of Christ's incarnation. Orthodox Christians enter the Church through three closely connected sacraments: baptism, chrismation, and the Eucharist. The Eucharist is the pinnacle of the Christian life. It unites baptized Christians to Christ and reminds them throughout the cycle of feasting and fasting that faith encompasses every aspect of life, from birth to death.

Chapter 8
Icons

IN THIS CHAPTER

- A confession of faith
- Veneration
- Liturgical art

The first thing that strikes a visitor to an Orthodox church is the presence of dozens of icons, with their rich profusion of colors and shapes. Icons are much more than a Bible for the illiterate. They are simultaneously a confession of faith, a prayer, a window into heaven, a liturgical object, a symbol of the Christian vocation, and an art in their own right.

The lines and colors that make up these sacred images are deeply symbolic. The word icon means image in Greek. With their multiple meanings, icons are both unique to and ubiquitous within Orthodoxy.[23]

Most people instinctively identify icons with Orthodoxy. Icons are a sign of its growth and influence. They can also bring Christians together, as we saw in 2004 when the Icon of the Mother of God of Kazan, which was particularly venerated in Russia and had long been kept in the Pope's private chapel, was returned to Moscow.

| A confession of faith

The Orthodox Church does not only confess its faith in words. Its faith is also expressed through symbols that embody a dual material and sacred reality. Icons are far more than just church decorations or devotional images intended to evoke an emotional response. According to the Seventh Ecumenical Council (Nicaea, 787), icons are at the heart of the definition of the Orthodox faith in Christ's divinity and humanity.

The iconoclastic controversy that rocked Byzantium in the eighth century is best understood as the continuation of the theological debates that emerged after the previous ecumenical councils. Icons of Christ, the Mother of God, and the saints became the focus of a conflict that tore the Empire apart. Iconoclasts believed that God cannot be represented, and that icons should therefore be destroyed. Iconodules, on the other hand, defended icons and their place in the life of the Church. Behind this apparently simplistic controversy lay an essential theological issue: the reality of Christ's human nature united to His divine nature. The fact that both Judaism and Islam prohibit any figurative depiction of God was doubtless another contributing factor.

The controversy first broke out in 726, when Emperor Leo III the Isaurian (717-741) ordered the persecution of the iconodules. It ended only when Empress Irene (797-803) took the throne. The iconodules'

---

23 Ouspensky, Leonid & Lossky, Vladimir, *The Meaning of Icons* (St. Vladimir's Seminary Press, 1999).

position was affirmed by the council of Nicaea in 787, which declared that icons should remain in the churches to be venerated. Saint John of Damascus (ca. 675-749) and Saint Theodore the Studite (759-856) were the two great defenders of icons during this period. For Saint John of Damascus in particular, the Old Testament prohibition on the depiction of God, the second of the Ten Commandments (Exodus 20:1-4) remains valid, but since the incarnation of Christ, God can be contemplated in a human form. Christ's incarnation profoundly altered the relationship between God and Creation.

A second wave of persecution began in 815 under the fervent iconoclast Emperor Leo V the Armenian (813-820) and lasted until 843. In that same year, Empress Theodora (842-867) permanently reestablished the veneration of icons. The Orthodox liturgical calendar commemorates this event on the first Sunday of Great Lent, the Sunday of the Triumph of Orthodoxy, which is marked by processions in which the clergy and faithful carry icons.

> *I do not worship matter, I worship the God of matter, who became matter for my sake, and deigned to inhabit matter, who worked out my salvation through matter. I will not cease from honoring that matter which works my salvation. I venerate it, though not as God. How could God be born out of lifeless things? And if God's body is God by its union with him, it is changeless. The nature of God remains the same as before, the flesh created in time is brought to life by a logical and reasoning soul.*
>
> Saint John of Damascus

Veneration

From a theological perspective, icons are justified by Christ's incarnation, but they also carry a message: the sanctified person portrayed is central to the reality of the icon. Icons tell us about God and are one of the ways that the Christian faith is passed on. They describe the key figures through whom salvation is offered to humanity. This educational function does not diminish their liturgical significance, however.

One of the iconoclasts' main accusations was that the veneration of icons was a form of idolatry. Today, Orthodox Christians still prominently display icons on the walls of both their churches and their homes. Icons are also placed on the iconostasis, which marks the boundary between the sanctuary (altar) and the nave in Orthodox church architecture. Orthodox Christians pray, light candles, prostrate themselves, and light incense before icons.

To understand their attachment to and veneration of these sacred images, we must first understand the underlying theological reasons for these expressions of piety. At this point, it is essential to make a clear distinction that was a major topic of discussion at the Seventh Ecumenical Council. Orthodox Christians do not worship the material of the icon – the wood, the pigments, or the colors. They venerate the person represented in the icon; worship is reserved for God alone. An icon is a symbol that depicts its subject using a very specific set of traditional techniques and exclusively natural materials.

The distinction between worship and veneration is extremely important because it avoids the misunderstanding that developed between the Christian East and West. The Greek term *proskynèsis* (veneration) was translated as *adoratio* (worship) in the Latin version of the Acts of the council of 787, blurring this distinction which had already been clearly articulated by Leontius of Neapolis in the mid-sixth century: "We do not make obeisance to the nature of wood, but we revere and do obeisance to Him who was crucified on the Cross..." The confusion introduced by the Latin translations of the council documents led Charlemagne (768-814) to reject them entirely.

Creating an icon

1. Preparing the support
Icons are usually painted on a wooden board, which can be any size and made from any kind of wood. The surface to be painted is coated with hot hide glue and then covered with a cloth soaked in the glue. It is then coated with gesso, a mixture of hide glue and whiting powder. Once it has dried and been sanded, it is ready for use.

2. Making the initial sketch
The iconographer sketches out his or her design.

3. **Applying gold**
Gold can be applied in limited areas or as the background of the icon

4. **Painting**
Naturally pigmented egg tempera paints are always used. The iconographer starts by applying the darkest colors before adding lighter colors.

5. **Adding the inscription**
The name of the person or event portrayed is written on the icon, to ensure it can be identified.

6. **Blessing**
Once the icon has dried and been varnished with a linseed oil mixture, it is placed in the church for forty days to bless it. At the end of the forty days, the priest reads a prayer to consecrate it for spiritual and liturgical use.

Liturgical art

Icons

Icons are an integral part of Orthodox liturgy. The first Christian art, which developed during the era of Roman persecutions, was an art of the catacombs. Iconography only began to blossom after the conversion of the Empire, developing its definitive vocabulary in the sixth century. The Ravenna mosaics offer a stunning example of this period. The encaustic paintings that survived the iconoclastic controversy provided the models for Byzantine classicism. The ninth and tenth century icons preserved at the Monastery of Saint Catherine in the Sinai and the first mosaics of the Hagia Sophia in Constantinople are some of the best examples of this period. Icons became more lifelike in the eleventh century under the Komnenos dynasty, gaining a spiritual depth seen in the renowned icon of the Virgin of Tenderness, frequently referred to as the Virgin of Vladimir. During the same period, with the exception of Ethiopia, the Oriental Churches that had left the Byzantine fold experienced relative artistic stagnation.

Both portable and mural iconography experienced a dramatic

expansion under the Palaiologos dynasty in the thirteenth and fourteenth centuries. As it grew increasingly expressive and historical, iconographic representation also became profoundly theological. This artistic renaissance accompanied a broader spiritual and cultural revival within the Byzantine commonwealth. Monks and iconographers from Mount Athos traveled through the Peloponnese, Epirus, Macedonia, and Kosovo and northwards to the plains of the Danube.

A distinctively Russian form of religious art emerged in the twelfth century. As the fourteenth century gave way to the fifteenth, Moscow adopted the hesychastic aesthetic under the influence of Theophanos the Greek. His disciple Andrei Rublev (1360-1430), the painter of the famous icon of the Trinity that depicts the hospitality of Abraham, achieved astoundingly pure luminosity. Their legacy was carried on by Dionysus the iconographer, who set the tone for the next two centuries of Russian iconography. In the Mediterranean world, in the sixteenth century, Crete became the school and inspiration for Greek, Romanian, Serbian, and Syrian painters including Michael Damaskinos (1530-1593) and Domenikos Theotokopoulos (1541-1614), better known as El Greco.

In the early modern period, westernized Orthodox iconography entered a decline parallel to that of Orthodox theology. The theological revival of the early twentieth century was accompanied by an iconographic revival. Leonid Ouspensky (1902-1987) in Paris and Photios Kontoglou (1895-1965) in Athens were the theoretical and practical pioneers of the movement, which today is represented by iconographers like the Monk Zenon in Russia and Stamatis Skliris in Greece. Contemporary iconography, however, remains dominated by the work of Fr. Grégoire Krug (d. 1969), which is found mainly in the Paris region but is known worldwide.

Other types of figurative art also exist within Orthodoxy, including Georgian cloisonné enamels and Armenian sculpted crosses *(khatchkar)*. The Orthodox tradition also includes a full range of liturgical handicrafts, from embroidery to bell casting. However, only liturgical music explicitly engages the same theological register as iconography.

Orthodox church architecture

History

The first Christian places of worship were found in private homes. In the fourth century, churches were built as basilicas, inspired by Roman architecture. Basilicas are rectangular in shape. Orthodox churches generally face east, towards the rising sun. The Church of the Nativity in Bethlehem is typical of the basilica style of the Constantinian era. Churches gradually changed shape over the centuries, with domes appearing in Constantinople and Anatolia in the early fifth century. The Hagia Sophia in Constantinople dates from this architectural period.

Starting in the seventh and eighth centuries, churches were increasingly built in the shape of a cross, with the bulk of their volume concentrated around the dome. The eleventh century church in the Greek monastery of Hosios Loukas is the most characteristic surviving example of this period. Today, Orthodox churches without domes are rare, although small basilicas are still built around the Black Sea and in northern Greece. Church architecture remained relatively unchanged over the second half of the first millennium, with the exception of the appearance of lateral chapels like those seen at the Chora Church in Istanbul (1321).

Serbia is home to a distinctive style of Orthodox church that draws on both Eastern and Western medieval architectural elements. An outstanding example of this tradition is found at the Monastery of the Mother of God in Studenica (twelfth – thirteenth centuries). The brick and stone churches typical of much of Romania were a later development, dating from the fourteenth century. Icons adorn the outside as well as the inside of some Romanian churches, such as the fifteenth century church of Voronet monastery in northern Romania.

The churches of Mistra, Meteora, Ohrid, Gracanica, and Tarnovo are among the jewels of Orthodoxy. But none has the dramatic intensity of the Chora Church of the Savior in Constantinople. The church was built close against the city walls and rebuilt shortly before the fall of the city. Its tympanum celebrates "Christ the land of the living," perhaps a premonition of the fate of the city.

Structure

Orthodox churches are usually built in the shape of a square cross. They are almost always topped with a dome, which in Russia took on the shape of an onion. The faithful usually stand throughout the service as a sign of Christ's resurrection. Due to this connection between standing and the Resurrection, kneeling is prohibited on Sundays and between Pascha and Pentecost. In Orthodox Churches, the narthex (vestibule) opens onto the nave, which is separated by an iconostasis from the sanctuary, where the altar is located.

On the altar, the gospel is laid on top of the *antimension*, a piece of cloth bearing an image of Christ before he was laid in the tomb. During the divine liturgy, the Gospel is moved to the side and the *antimension* is unfolded to receive the chalice and paten for the consecration of the bread and wine. Originally, the *antimension* allowed the celebration of the Eucharist when no consecrated altar was available. It is vitally important for pastoral care in times of war and persecution since it enables the Divine Liturgy to be served anywhere. The altar itself simultaneously represents the table of the Mystical Supper, the heavenly altar, the throne of the Trinity, and the tomb of Christ. It is consecrated during a special ceremony by the insertion of relics that are sealed inside it. It is then washed and anointed with oil, echoing the sacraments of baptism and chrismation that prepare Christians to receive the Eucharist. An *artophorion*, a container in which parcels of the Eucharist that will be used for Communion for the sick are kept, stands on the altar. The parcels placed in it are consecrated on Holy Thursday.

On the left of the altar is another table, called the *prothesis*. This is where the bread and wine are prepared for the celebration of the Divine Liturgy. The chalice and paten are placed on this table. Wine mixed with water is poured into the chalice. The bread used for the liturgy must be leavened and marked with a seal showing the anagram of Christ the Victor, IC XC NI KA; a triangle representing the Mother of God; and nine smaller triangles that represent the different orders of sanctity (angels, apostles, holy priests, martyrs, etc.). During the prayer of the *proskomidia*, which is said at the *prothesis*, the priest or bishop who is celebrating the liturgy uses a tiny lance to place small portions of bread to commemorate the names of the faithful that are given to him. The way he places the bread during this prayer represents the world centered around Christ. Once the priest has finished commemorating the living and the dead, he places the *asterisk* and three veils that entirely cover the paten and the chalice on the paten above the central piece of bread, called the lamb.

The iconostasis is a wall of icons between the nave and the sanctuary. The celebrant can enter the altar through two side doors, known as the deacon's doors, and one central double door, known as the royal doors. The first iconostases were about waist high, but the number of rows of icons has increased over time. Greek churches generally have two or three rows of icons, while in the Slavic tradition, the iconostasis can be much taller. Only ordained clergy may enter the altar through the royal doors.

Orthodox chant

Throughout the Christian East, tradition prohibits the use of musical instruments in the church, with the exception of a few percussion instruments in Ethiopia. Orthodox Church music is entirely vocal. It is collective, using the ancient practice of chanting in unison with varying levels of intensity. In keeping with the Orthodox practice of baptizing cultures, Orthodox liturgical music reflects both ancient traditions and different national styles. The Syriac, Coptic, and Ethiopian traditions have developed a profound artistry that rivals the Byzantine tradition, which is also the ancestor of Slavonic church music. All of these traditions feature a level of technicality and complexity comparable with that of Western Gregorian chant.

Byzantine music is inseparable from the liturgy. Serving as a chanter is considered a form of ministry. Many of the theologians who wrote the texts of Orthodox hymns were also composers. Like other Orthodox liturgical arts, Byzantine music attained its classical form in the fourteenth century with Ioannis Koukouzelis (1280-1360) before experiencing a decline and a later revival. A liturgical music reform was launched in Constantinople in the nineteenth century by Bishop Chrysanthus and completed in Athens in the twentieth century by Simon Karas (1905-1999). The greatest representative of this ressourcement, Lycourgos Angelopoulos (1941-2014), guided the work of Anatoly Grindenko in Russia during the same period. Angelopoulos and Grindenko shared three goals: first, to restore a living understanding of the written tradition; second, to eliminate western influence from musical praxis; and finally, to restore the original liturgical and spiritual dimension of Orthodox music.

Much like icons, Byzantine and Slavonic chant are representative of Orthodoxy and its contemporary challenges. Orthodox music draws on a comprehensive theological vision, including the definition of human beings as instruments of grace, the primacy of ascesis and communion, and the centrality of the tangible experience of God.

| Key points

- Icons are the ultimate symbol of Orthodoxy. They are a powerful confession of faith in the union of the human and the divine in Christ, which allows the representation of God in the person of Jesus. This position was supported by the Seventh Ecumenical Council (Nicaea, 787).

- Icons are not simply works of art. They are above all liturgical objects that are venerated by the faithful. This veneration is not a form of idolatry; it is directed to the person represented in the icon. Icons depict the holiness of their subjects.

- All forms of art are baptized through the baptism of cultures. Artistic excellence serves the glory of God. Orthodox liturgical music is unique, although its form varies in different countries. Orthodox tradition prohibits the use of musical instruments in worship because only the human voice can praise God with words.

Chapter 9
Spirituality

IN THIS CHAPTER

- Monasticism
- The theological revival of the twentieth century
- Major figures of contemporary Orthodoxy

Orthodox spirituality is based first and foremost on the monastic experience, asceticism, and prayer. Monasteries play an essential role in the flourishing of Orthodox communities. In Orthodoxy, spirituality is understood as a life in the Holy Spirit. In the words of the Apostle Paul,

> By contrast, the fruit of the Spirit is love, joy, peace, patience, kindness, generosity, faithfulness, gentleness, and self-control. There is no law against such things. And those who belong to Christ have crucified the flesh with its passions and desires. If we live by the Spirit, let us also be guided by the Spirit.
>
> Galatians 5:22

Orthodox spirituality is grounded in the experience of the Christian life and the application of the principles laid out in the Bible.

It is what has enabled the Orthodox Church to remain engaged with the world and thus a living Church. That vitality is particularly evident in the theological revival that developed over the course of the twentieth century, as the Church encountered modernity. Because Orthodoxy is a religion of incarnation, an embodied faith, the Christian life is rooted in the baptismal vocation of every Christian. Several major contemporary figures have left their imprint – and continue to make their mark – on a world thirsting for inspiration and renewal.

Monasticism

History

Monasticism is central to the life and growth of Orthodoxy. To better understand its importance, we need to start with its origins.

Orthodox monasticism first appeared in the Egyptian desert in the fourth century. As the era of persecution came to an end, the desire for total consecration to God remained strong. The martyrdom of blood gradually gave way to the "martyrdom of tears," a life entirely focused on God in a quest for spiritual perfection and in efforts to defend the faith. Its emergence would influence the future of the entire Church. Monasticism, both male and female, is considered the prophetic voice of the Church, fully focused on the coming of the Kingdom of God which is not of this world. Today, Mount Athos remains one of the leading monastic centers of the Orthodox world.

> **Mount Athos**
>
> *Located in the Macedonia region of northeastern Greece, Mount Athos is both a mountain and a peninsula. It is famous for its many Orthodox monasteries, some of them over a thousand years old. Today, Mount Athos is home to twenty historic monasteries as well as numerous hermitages, all placed under the jurisdiction of the Ecumenical Patriarchate. It is often referred to as the Holy Mountain. Monks from Greece and other traditionally Orthodox*

> countries like Romania, Bulgaria, Russia, Serbia, and Georgia live lives of extreme asceticism on the mountain. Mount Athos is officially organized as a monastic republic governed by a council of representatives of the twenty monasteries. This council is called the "Holy Community" and has a board known as the "Holy Epistasia." The communities of the Holy Mountain still follow the Julian Calendar. A rule established in 1045 and still in force today, known as the rule of avaton (literally "inaccessible") prohibits women from entering the peninsula because it is consecrated to the Virgin Mary.
>
> Mount Athos is home to many precious icons and ancient manuscripts.

| Origins and thought

The monastic movement began with men and women leaving society for the desert. Some lived as hermits or semi-hermits, while others formed communities with varying degrees of independence, but all sought to live the Gospel more deeply and fully. Saint Anthony the Great (251-356), who is considered the father of monasticism, took the Gospel very literally: "If you wish to be perfect, go, sell your possessions, and give the money to the poor, and you will have treasure in heaven; then come, follow me" (Matthew 19:21). The contemplative life recommended by Saint Anthony goes hand in hand with asceticism and prayer. Monasticism has profoundly influenced the Orthodox Church, from its liturgical development to its theology and its relationship with secular authority.

Ascesis

> The word "asceticism" comes from the Greek word for exercise and physical training. It came to mean training the soul to acquire the virtues by subjugating the body, but without divorcing the spiritual and material parts of the person. Ascesis is a struggle against the passions, which are defined as the temptations that turn us away from God. The body is put to the test by prayer and fasting. In the words of Christ: "But this kind does not come out except by prayer and fasting" (Matthew 17:21).

The ideal of monasticism is found in its name, which is derived from the Greek word *monos* (alone). This ideal is lived out in solitude and silence. Even in a community, the spiritual lives of monks and nuns are organized around the quiet of personal prayer. Liturgical services form the rhythm of monastic life. Within monastic communities, elders, known as *gerondes* in Greek and *startsi* in Russian, emerge. These elders guide and assist the other brothers and sisters to help them live out their vows as virtues: fasting and celibacy, chastity and poverty. In Orthodox monasticism, there are no distinctive orders, although different rules have existed: the rule of Pachomius (292-348), later reworked by Saint Benedict (480-547), and the best known, the rule of Saint Basil the Great (329-379).

Evagrius Ponticus (345-399) was the first to develop the beginnings of a doctrine on the passions and the concept of "pure prayer." His writings lay out a comprehensive spiritual anthropology of the relationship between human beings and God. Saint Makarios the Great (300-391), one of the greatest Desert Fathers of the fourth century, focused on the reality of the spiritual life based on the sacraments of baptism and the Eucharist. The union with God that is the goal of all spiritual life is a tangible, personal experience. Saint Simeon the New Theologian (949-1022) wrote in the same vein, highlighting that the Christian faith must be understood as the experience of the living Christ.

| Conversion

Conversion is an essential principle of Orthodox monasticism. It not only recognizes the weakness and limitations of human nature before God's omnipotence but also affirms the irresistible human inclination towards passions and sin, defined as turning away from the good. However, this understanding of human sinfulness is not an end in itself. It is also a call to conversion. The Greek word for conversion is *metanoia*, which also means repentance, but in a sense that is far more profound than a simple apology. In Orthodox monastic literature, it means a transformation of the self, an entire reorientation of the whole person, leaving egotism and self-centeredness behind to be recentered on the mystery of God's life-giving and radiant grace. Much monastic literature is dedicated to conversion and how to achieve it. Certain ascetic saints like Saint Silouan of Athos (1866) wrote about continual remembrance of death, while others like Saint John Climacus (579-649) wrote extensively on the virtues to acquire in order to turn away from evil. In *The Ladder of Divine Ascent*, Saint John Climacus lays out a path that leads upwards towards an encounter with God.

That encounter is at the heart of the monastic life. Monasticism is quite simply the vocation of all Christians lived with maximal intensity. Conversion, as taught by Orthodox monasticism, can be understood as an encounter between God and the human person. Orthodox theology refers to a "synergy," a collaboration in which the infinite love of God who seeks to save encounters the will of the person who wants to be saved. In the words of Saint John Climacus, "Repentance is a contract with God for a second life."

Metanoia is a transformative force that turns the passions into virtues by redirecting the death-bearing power of evil towards the life-giving actions of grace. It is followed by the contemplation of the divine (*theoria*) as the fruit of union with God.

| The Jesus Prayer

One of the "means" to conversion of the heart is the Jesus prayer. The Jesus prayer refers to the practice of using a prayer rope to repeat the simple prayer: "Lord Jesus Christ, Son of God, have mercy on me, a sinner." This prayer, also known as the "prayer of the heart," is characteristic of the spiritual vigor of Orthodox monasticism. For several centuries, it has also been embraced by the Orthodox faithful outside monasteries. Prayer of the heart is the mark of hesychasm because silence is the setting for prayer. It is a response to the Apostle Paul's call to "pray without ceasing" (1 Thessalonians 5:17). Repeating the Jesus prayer is not just a mantra or a method for prayer. It engages the entire person in order to unite the heart, which is the center of human nature, and the mind, the space of personal liberty. By uniting heart and mind, the believer unites himself or herself to the divine life by concentrating on the name of Jesus in prayer. Through grace, invoking the name of the second person of the Holy Trinity realizes His presence in the Church. In the fourteenth century, the Jesus prayer gave rise to an intense controversy that produced the hesychastic theology championed by Saint Gregory Palamas (1296-1359).

The way in which the Jesus prayer is recited involves the whole body, uniting words and breath. Christ reveals Himself through the prayer, bringing the joy and warmth of His presence, which the faithful must learn to recognize – hence the importance of spiritual direction. A particularly popular late nineteenth century work, *The Way of a Pilgrim*, offers a powerful account of the wanderings of a man seeking the prayer of the heart, aided only by the Bible and the *Philokalia*.

The Jesus prayer has become the mark not only of Orthodox monasticism but of Orthodox revival. Orthodox Christians are deeply attached to both, as demonstrated by the vast literature on the subject and the influence of certain monasteries such as the Monastery of Saint John the Baptist in England, known for the teachings of Saint Sophronius (Sakharov) of Essex (1896-1993). Saint Sophronius was largely responsible for the spread of the teachings of Saint Silouan of Athos, of whom he was a disciple.

| The twentieth century theological revival

The Orthodox theological revival was in many ways the product of the encounter between Eastern and Western Christianity, made possible by the turmoil that drove waves of Orthodox Christians into exile in the twentieth century. This revival grew out of the desire to rediscover the tradition of the early Church and the teachings of the Scripture and the Church Fathers. It sought not only to purge the western influences that had affected Orthodox theology in the second half of the second millennium but also to truly rediscover the original experience of Christianity by combining theology, spiritual life, and asceticism.

| The "Paris School" and the renewal of Russian theology

The Russian diaspora in France after the Revolution of 1917 bubbled with tremendous intellectual and theological energy. The diaspora was centered around the *"Institut de Théologie Orthodoxe Saint-Serge,"* founded in Paris in 1924. The "Paris School" brought the Russian intellectual elite into contact with the West, pushing it to undertake a profound reexamination of the elements that form the Orthodox tradition. These authors' works not only defended Orthodox positions but also sought to make them accessible to their new contacts, who had previously known very little about Eastern Christianity. According to scholars, the Paris School can be divided into four streams:

- The first stream focused on the Patristic revival. The neopatristic movement, sometimes called the "return to the Fathers," was the mark of the revival in contemporary Orthodox theology. This liberation from Western theological influence was led by figures like Fr. Georges Florovsky (1893-1979), Vladimir Lossky (1903-1958) and Fr. John Meyendorff (1926-1992) in France, as well as Fr. Dumitru Staniloae (1903-1993) in Romania and Fr. Justin Popovic (1894-1979) in Serbia.

- The second stream, which focused on liturgical questions, was spearheaded by Fr. Nicholas Afanasieff (1893-1966) and Rev. Alexander Schmemann (1921-1983). Their work highlighted the importance of the Eucharist in the life and organization of the Church.

- The third stream took a more purely historical and research-oriented approach to history, literature, and spirituality. Its best-known representative is Anton Kartashev (1875-1960).

- The fourth stream studied Russian thought and philosophy. Nikolai Berdyaev (1874-1948) was one of its leading figures.

Fr. Sergey Bulgakov (1871-1944), whose immense body of work and theological and intellectual engagement made him the leader of the "Paris School," belonged not to one but to all four of these streams.

Bulgakov was a professor of dogmatic theology at Saint-Serge and wrote a particularly vivid theological synthesis of the Orthodox tradition, although his doctrine of *sophia*, an intermediary between God and humanity, drew harsh criticism from Vladimir Lossky and other Russian emigré theologians.

> **Saint Sergius Orthodox Theological Institute**
>
> *The Saint Sergius Orthodox Theological Institute was founded in the 1920s on the site of a German Lutheran Church in northern Paris, thanks to the energetic efforts of Metropolitan Eulogius Georgievsky (1868-1946). The campus, which is still home to both the school and a parish church, was the spiritual training center for Russian emigré clergy who had found refuge in France. The Institute very quickly began to participate in inter-Christian and ecumenical endeavors. It started to transition to French-language instruction in the 1960s with the arrival of the French theologian Olivier Clément (1921-2009).*

In the Greek world

In the Greek world, the twentieth century theological revival took on a very different form. It was essentially founded by major figures like Nikos Nissiotis (1924-1986), John Romanides (1927-2001), Christos Yannaras (1935-2024) and Metropolitan John Zizioulas (1931-2023). The movement was animated by the publication of journals like *Synoro* (1964-1967) and later *Synaxi* (founded in 1982 by Panayiotis Nellas). All of these authors were central figures in the "neopatristic synthesis" and contributed to the Paris School revival, the rediscovery of a sense of tradition and of the place of the people of God in the Church in the light of the Eucharist, and of an ascetic spirituality based on the *Philokalia*.

The Greek world was also marked by the *Zoè* (Life) movement, a semi-monastic movement dedicated to teaching, preaching, youth groups, and publishing since the early twentieth century. The vigor of Orthodoxy in Greece today owes much to the movement's activities. In the 1960s, internal conflict led to the creation of another organization, *Soter* (Savior). However, the movement was accused of collusion with the Athenian military junta in the 1960s and was severely undermined after the fall of the regime in 1974.

The "return to the Fathers"

As strange as it may seem, the "return to the Fathers" is closely linked to Orthodoxy's encounter with the Christian West, and particularly inter-Christian and ecumenical dialogue – even though the movement sought to free Orthodox theology from western influence. At the same time, this introspective approach to Orthodox tradition led to the emergence of a form of deeply conservative traditionalism within Orthodoxy. Some authors have criticized the neopatristic synthesis, accusing it of devaluing biblical studies, lack of historical research, ceding to the temptation to polarize Eastern and Western Christianity, and being completely disconnected from contemporary issues.

However, the promotion of the teaching of the Church Fathers has enabled the translation of an enormous patristic corpus into modern languages, highlighting not only their teachings but also the relevance, not to say universality, of their writings and providing crucial points of contact with intellectuals, particularly Catholic scholars such as Yves Congar (1904-1995) and Henri-Irénée Marrou (1904-1977).

Major figures of contemporary Orthodoxy

Of the many individuals who embody the energy and renewal of Orthodoxy today, three are particularly emblematic: Saint Maria Skobtsova, also known as Saint Maria of Paris, Ecumenical Patriarch Bartholomew of Constantinople, and Metropolitan Georges of Mount Lebanon. All of them represent, in their own unique way, one of the aspects of Eastern Christianity: holiness, unity, and mission.

Saint Maria Skobtsova (1891-1945)

Saint Maria Skobtsova was born Elizaveta Yurievna Pilenko in 1891 in Riga, now the capital of Latvia, which was then part of the Russian Empire. Elizaveta developed a fascination with the arts at a very early age. In 1910, when still in her teens, she married the socialist intellectual Dimitri Kuzmin-Karaviev, who shared her love of literature. Their marriage did not last and they soon divorced. After the Russian Revolution broke out in 1917, Elizaveta emigrated with her second husband, Daniel Skobtsov, who had served in the White Russian Army.

They initially fled to Constantinople, before arriving in Paris in 1923 with three children, Gaiana, George, and Anastasia. Anastasia died in 1926. A few years later, Elizaveta became a nun, taking the name Maria in honor of Saint Mary of Egypt. During this period, she worked with the Russian Christian student youth movement and more broadly with the large Russian immigrant community that was streaming into Paris. Mother Maria opened her house at 77 rue de Lourmel in southern Paris to everyone, especially the needy, going to the Les Halles market every day to find food for hungry families.[24] Starting in June 1941, she actively aided prisoners arrested by the Nazis and organized the distribution of packages to prisoners and their families. She also unhesitatingly helped protect Jews from Nazi persecution, providing them with baptismal certificates so they could leave the occupied zone for the free zone in the south. During the Vel d'Hiv roundup of July 1942, she saved three or four children from arrest and deportation.

Mother Maria was arrested by the Gestapo in 1943 along with her son George, her secretary Theodore Pianov, and Father Dimitri Klepinin. She was then deported to Ravensbrück, where she was prisoner number 19 263. Many stories from her fellow prisoners in the concentration camp tell of how she continued to help the weak, resisting dehumanization and hatred with all her strength. She died on March 31, 1945 – Holy Saturday on the Orthodox calendar that year – after taking the place of a young Jewish woman who had been selected for the gas chamber. She was canonized as a martyr by the Ecumenical Patriarchate of Constantinople in 2004 and is also recognized as Righteous Among the Nations by the State of Israel. Today, a Parisian street that opens onto rue de Lourmel, where she lived, bears her name: "rue Mère-Marie-Skobtsov."

---

24 *Cf.* Maria Skobtsova, *Essential Writings* (Orbis Books, 2002)

Ecumenical Patriarch Bartholomew

Ecumenical Patriarch Bartholomew was born Dimitrios Archondonis on February 29, 1940, in the village of Haghioi Theodoroi, on the Mediterranean island of Imbros (now İmroz or Gökçeada, in Türkiye). The young Dimitrios, who was from a humble background, attended school on the island before leaving for Istanbul to attend high school. After graduation, he immediately enrolled in the theological school of Halki, graduating in 1961. In August of the same year, he was ordained a deacon by his mentor and spiritual father Metropolitan Meliton of Imbros, taking the name Bartholomew. Before continuing his studies abroad, he spent two years completing his Turkish military service. Once his military service was finished, he continued his studies at the Pontifical Oriental Institute in Rome and then the Ecumenical Institute Bossey in Switzerland and the University of Munich (Germany) before defending his doctoral thesis at the Gregorian University in Rome.

After returning from his years abroad, the future patriarch gradually took on new responsibilities, initially as head of the theological school of Halki, which closed in 1971 under pressure from the Turkish authorities. Ecumenical Patriarch Athenagoras (1948-1972) then appointed him to a key role at the Phanar – another name for the Ecumenical Patriarchate, named for the Istanbul neighborhood where it is located. Ordained a priest in 1969, he was made a bishop in 1973 with the title Metropolitan of Philadelphia. He later became the secretary of Ecumenical Patriarch Dimitrios (1972-1991), eventually succeeding him in 1991.

Ecumenical Patriarch Bartholomew has been at the helm of global Orthodoxy for over three decades. As Rev. John Chryssavgis highlights in his recent biography of the Patriarch, he plays a key role on the global stage.[25] He works tirelessly to achieve Orthodox unity despite the difficult situation faced by the Ecumenical Patriarchate in Türkiye. In addition to the tragic decrease in the number of Greek Orthodox in the country and the Turkish authorities' refusal to grant the patriarchate any legal status, the continued closure of

---

25 Chryssavgis, John, *Bartholomew: Apostle and Visionary* (Thomas Nelson, 2016)

the theological school of Halki undermines the very existence of these communities in their own homeland. Despite these struggles at home, it was thanks to the determination of Ecumenical Patriarch Bartholomew that the Holy and Great Council of the Orthodox Church was finally held in 2016.

Ecumenical Patriarch Bartholomew's actions also extend beyond the Orthodox Church. He is best known for his commitment to the environment, which dates to before the 1990s. The close connection between his environmental thought and commitments and his spiritual vocabulary has earned him the nickname of the "green Patriarch." He has even inspired the "spiritual ecology" championed by Pope Francis and was mentioned in the 2015 papal encyclical *Laudato Si*.

> *It is important to emphasize that the concern of the Ecumenical Patriarchate for the natural environment has not emerged from the contemporary ecological crisis. This crisis was the occasion and opportunity for the promotion of the ecological principles and values of Orthodoxy. The very life of the Church is an applied ecology, a true respect for the environment. The ecumenical and ascetic ethos, the simplification of life, the civilization of the person and love dominate here.*
>
> Ecumenical Patriarch Bartholomew

Ecumenical Patriarch Bartholomew works tirelessly to bring Christian Churches together in a true quest for unity. These ecumenical endeavors have been encouraged by his numerous meetings with Pope Francis. Keenly aware of the vital role that religious leaders play in promoting peace, he also strives to foster interreligious dialogue. We owe to Ecumenical Patriarch Bartholomew these words:

> *Despite the many challenges of our time, despite the fear of those who content themselves with the clash of civilizations, despite the rise of religious intolerance, fundamentalism, hatred, and anti-Semitism, we should stay firm and promote an ethos of dialogue and solidarity. We try – in faithfulness to our respective faith traditions*

> – *to promote the creation of bridges respectful of the beliefs of the others in a spirit of peace and solidarity.*
>
> Ecumenical Patriarch Bartholomew

Metropolitan Georges of Mount Lebanon

All too often, we forget that Orthodoxy is not only Greek or Slavic. It also has a strong presence in the Arab world, alongside Islam and other Eastern Christian confessions. Metropolitan Georges of Mount Lebanon is emblematic of the ways in which Orthodoxy offers a bridge between the different religious communities in the region.

Metropolitan Georges Khodr was born on July 6, 1923, in Tripoli, Lebanon's second-largest city. He studied law at Saint Joseph University of Beirut with plans to become a diplomat, graduating in 1944. On March 16, 1942, he founded the Orthodox Youth Movement along with fifteen other law and medical students. The organization sparked a revival in the Greek Orthodox Patriarchate of Antioch, revitalizing parish life with student Bible study groups and a new commitment to monasticism. Social, ecumenical, and interreligious engagement were the hallmarks of the movement. On November 11, 1943, Georges participated in a peaceful protest against the French colonial government, which opposed the Lebanese people's claims to independence. The protest ended in bloodshed when shots were fired at the protesters, killing eleven.

In the early 1950s, the future metropolitan left Lebanon to study at the Saint Sergius Orthodox Theological Institute in Paris. He earned a bachelor's degree in theology in 1952 before returning to Lebanon, where he was ordained a priest two years later. He was quickly noted for his qualities as both a theologian and a preacher, traveling throughout the diocese of Tripoli. He was eventually elected a bishop on February 15, 1970, and was ordained as Metropolitan of Mount Lebanon. In addition to his pastoral work, he was intensely committed to education, serving as a professor of Arabic culture at the Lebanese University and teaching pastoral theology at the Saint

John of Damascus School of Theology at the University of Balamand. Metropolitan Georges was a pioneer of ecumenical dialogue with other Christian confessions and the author of numerous works on the relationship between Orthodoxy and Islam, a religion with which he was intimately familiar as an expert on the Quran. His approach to dialog with the Muslim world was centered on the need to recognize God's work in action, using the unique approach of the Church Fathers.

| Key points

- Orthodox spirituality can be described as a spirituality of conversion. A person converts to Christianity, just as he or she continues to convert throughout his or her life by turning away from sin and choosing holiness. Conversion is also repentance. Monasticism, with its rules, its rigor, and its consecration, is the greatest example of repentance.

- Orthodox spirituality is intensely alive, constantly revisiting its relationship to tradition and its origins. Its monastic life, with its historic tradition and living spiritual experience, is flourishing. Monasteries play a central role in Orthodox life as places of pilgrimage and retreat, crystallizing knowledge and prayer as a single reality.

- Orthodoxy's encounter with the West fostered a theological revival based on a return to the Church Fathers as the source of the Orthodox tradition.

- Contemporary Orthodoxy has been marked by three great figures:
    o Saint Maria Skobtsova and her martyrdom;
    o Ecumenical Patriarch Bartholomew and his commitment to Orthodox unity and the protection of the environment;
    o Metropolitan Georges of Mount Lebanon and his spirit of dialogue.

FURTHER READING

Reference works on Orthodox history and theology

Alfeyev, Metropolitan Hilarion, *1: Orthodox Christianity Volume I: The History and Canonical Structure of the Orthodox Church* (St. Vladimir's Seminary Press, 2011)

Bartholomew, Ecumenical Patriarchate, *Encountering the Mystery: Understanding Orthodox Christianity Today* (Doubleday, 2008).

Bulgakov, Sergius, *The Church of Orthodoxy* (St. Vladimir's Seminary Press, 1997).

Clément, Olivier, *The Church of Orthodoxy* (Chelsea House, 2001)

Clément, Olivier, *Roots of Christian Mysticism: Texts from Patristic Era with Commentary* (New City Press, 1996).

Lossky, Vladimir, *The Mystical Theology of the Eastern Church* (St. Vladimir's Seminary Press, 1997).

Meyendorff, John, *Byzantine Theology: Historical Trends and Doctrinal Themes* (Fordham University Press, 1999)?

Meyendorff, John, *Orthodox Church: Its Past and Its Role in the World Today* (St. Vladimir's Seminary Press, 1981).

Pelikan, Jaroslav, *The Christian Tradition: A History of the Development of Doctrine*, 5 vols. (University of Chicago Press 1971–1990).

Schmemann, Alexander, *The Historical Road of Eastern Orthodoxy* (St. Vladimir's Seminary Press, 1997).

Ware, Kallistos, *The Orthodox Church: Second Edition* (Penguin Books, 1993).

Specialized studies

Bentley, David & Chryssavgis, John (ed.), *For the Life of the World. Toward a Social Ethos of the Orthodox Church* (Holy Cross Orthodox Press, 2020).

Chaillot, Christine (ed.), *The Dialogue Between the Eastern Orthodox and Oriental Orthodox Churches* (Volos Academy Publications, 2016).

Chryssavgis, John, *Bartholomew: Apostle and Visionary* (Thomas Nelson, 2016).

Gallatin, Matthew, *Thirsting for God in a Land of Shallow Wells* (Ancient Faith Publishing, 2002).

Grabar, Andre, *Byzantine Painting* (Rizzoli Intl Pubns, 1979).

Meyendorff, John, *Imperial Unity and Christian Divisions: The Church 450-680 A.D.* (St. Vladimir's Seminary Press, 2011).

Runciman, Steven, *The Fall of Constantinople 1453* (Cambridge University Press, 1990).

Shanbour, Rev. Michael, *Know the Faith. A Handbook for Orthodox Christians and Inquirers* (Ancient Faith Publications, 2016).

Yannaras, Christos. *The Freedom of Morality* (St. Vladimir's Seminary Press, 2004).

More specialized recommendations can be found in the footnotes.

www.ingramcontent.com/pod-product-compliance
Lightning Source LLC
LaVergne TN
LVHW020933090426
835512LV00020B/3330